DÁLVI
SIX YEARS IN THE ARCTIC TUNDRA

Laura Galloway

DÁLVI

SIX YEARS IN THE
ARCTIC TUNDRA

ALLEN&UNWIN

First published in Great Britain in 2021 by Allen & Unwin

Portions of this book appeared previously in *Intelligent Life* magazine

The Law of Jante excerpt on pp.96-97 is taken from *A Fugitive Crosses His Tracks* by Aksel Sandemose (A.A. Knopf, 1936)

Allen & Unwin
c/o Atlantic Books
Ormond House
26–27 Boswell Street
London WC1N 3JZ

Phone: 020 7269 1610
Fax: 020 7430 0916
Email: UK@allenandunwin.com
Web: www.allenandunwin.com/uk

A CIP catalogue record for this book is available from the British Library.

Hardback ISBN 978 1 91163 067 8
E-Book ISBN 978 1 76087 325 7

Printed in Great Britain by TJ Books Limited

10 9 8 7 6 5 4 3 2 1

For Jonathan

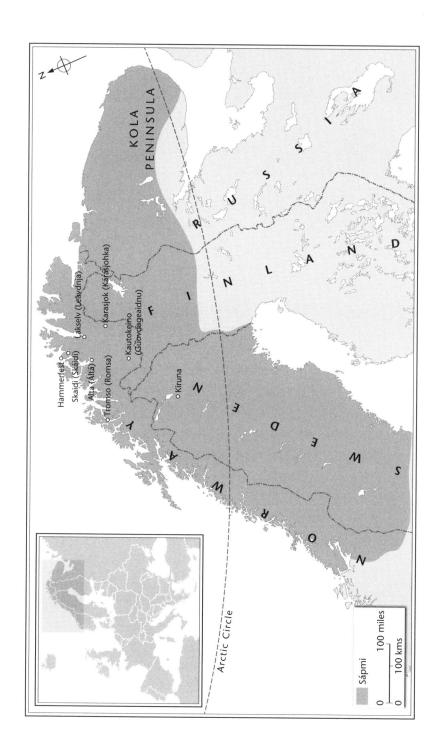

KOLA
PENINSULA

RUSSIA

FINLAND

Hammerfest
Skaidi (Skáidi)
Lakselv (Leavdnja)
Karasjok (Kárášjohka)
Alta (Álta)
Kautokeino
(Guovdageaidnu)
Tromso (Romsa)

Kiruna

NORWAY

SWEDEN

Arctic Circle

Sápmi

100 miles
0
100 kms
0

AUTHOR'S NOTE

Many, but not all, of the names and some key identifying details of the central individuals about whom I write in this book have been changed in the interest of privacy and anonymity. There are no fictional or composite people or events. *Dálvi* is based on many years of notes, diaries, letters and my memories and recollections. In the editing process, I have tried my best to respect Sámi culture by employing a Sámi reader for checking of key facts, spellings and impressions, yet it cannot be underscored enough that *Dálvi* is singularly a product of my urban, outsider lens and experiences in this particular culture, rather than an insider's view or perspective.

INTRODUCTION

It is minus fifteen Fahrenheit the first time I arrive in the Arctic, in *dálvi*, the Northern Sámi word for winter. A giant LCD screen at Sweden's Kiruna airport displays the temperature. As I step off the plane, it is not the snow or the cold or the bleakness that gives me pause. It is the utter silence, muffling even the idling jet engine of the plane. My cheeks bloom red from the brittle cold as I wait for a taxi next to a sign indicating a parking spot for sled dogs. This is the farthest place imaginable from my home in New York, in both temperature and ambience.

The air is completely still and lead-like with the cold, as if words might shatter if spoken. As we drive through the night to my hotel, I'm oblivious to the towering Scots pines and Norwegian spruce that dot the forlorn roadsides and would appear with the golden pink light of morning, laden with layers and layers of snow, creating towering sculptures of spun candyfloss. The beauty is singular, and it is also deceptive; this is, too, a place of dark and endless nights, of bitter cold and of survival.

The Arctic north in winter is a great void, which is perhaps why I am so drawn to it. In its nothingness, there is no chaos, no ambiguity; there is nothing to be done except to *be there*, swallowed by the enormousness of one's surroundings, a bleakness which can either foster a sense of retreat or inspire possibility, depending on your state of mind and what you need most at that moment.

I am filled with the sense of aloneness that has travelled with me longer than I can remember, which is a part of me. But in the sting of the cold, I also feel something foreign and unfamiliar, and which I thought had been lost to me long ago: a sense of wonder.

1

UNRAVELLED

Freezing cold and tired, I am holding on to a long green tarp, alongside a handful of others, guiding reindeer into an enormous holding enclosure in a remote part of the Norwegian Arctic. A giant buttery moon lies flat against the hard blue twilight sky, so low you feel as if you could easily touch it. It illuminates everything: from the jumpy reindeer moving en masse, a blinding flurry of hooves and poop and antlers, to my warm breath hitting the rimy cold night sky in plumes like a smoker with a phantom cigarette. As I look up at the moon, toes numb in my muddy boots from having stood for what feels like hours waiting for the herders to bring the reindeer in from the tundra, I am struck by the absolute insanity and marvel of life, and of the improbable twists and turns in our stories that we could never begin to imagine.

One year ago, a Saturday night would not have involved standing on the frozen expanse of the Finnmark plateau with a family of Sámi herders, watching steaming blood being scooped out of a reindeer carcass as it's field-dressed by a grunting Sámi man named Odd Hætta with a giant knife. One year ago, I would have been walking through Union Square in New York on my way to a progressively boozy dinner with friends, spending hours talking about their work and my media job, and did you read *such* and *such* in the *New Yorker*, and what show was on at MoMA or what was happening in the increasingly worrying political landscape. And, of course, there would have been talk of relationship problems – and there were always problems – or money problems and how *busy* everyone was. And then the evening would have slowly unravelled, everyone growing louder and more maudlin, until it was over, faded into a history of Saturdays just like every other one that came before it, followed by a sharp hangover the next day, a raft of emails and stress and worries about everything back in full view in an endless cycle.

Those days were now far behind me, a distant memory of the person I was, tucked away like the dozens of utterly useless high-heeled shoes that sat with all my other earthly possessions in a storage area some two thousand miles away in Manhattan, collecting dust and losing relevance. In my old life, tomorrow I would be heading to City Bakery for an iced coffee, with crippling anxiety about the Monday to come and how I would hang on one more day in a life that was becoming unmanageable to an extent of which no one around me was really aware, unless you happened to be the lucky recipient of a spectacular late-night Laura Galloway Ambien and red-wine phone call.

I was breaking open and falling apart, and to reveal this weakness and vulnerability to anyone might have caused me to die of shame. But the universe seemed to have plans for me, ones that would take me outside of everything I knew, and everything that I thought made me *me*, to a place where I now think nothing of not showering for three days straight, and Saturday involves helping chop wood for a fence-post, or cutting reeds to dry and braid into shoes for the brittle winter to come, or smoking reindeer meat in a tent called a *lávvu* while drinking bitter black coffee, the smoke clinging to my hair and clothing and settling into my pores. This is a place where you have to be with yourself because there are no distractions. Only work and nature and time.

*

It all started with a test.

I was at a conference where I received a DNA test in my gift bag. When I got home, I took the test, sent it off and forgot about it, until the result arrived and I was completely bewildered to read its findings: that I shared some portion of extremely ancient DNA with the Sámi people and the Basques, the former being the indigenous Arctic inhabitants of the north of Norway, Sweden, Finland and the Kola Peninsula of Russia. It also indicated that I was nearly 100 per cent Northern European, and showed a picture of what I thought looked oddly like a left-leaning penis: Norway and Sweden on a map. My other 2 per cent was something equally far flung – Yakutian or Siberian: I can no longer remember which. I didn't understand that either, and wondered if I had a particularly adventurous great-great-great-grandmother somewhere, an idea I relished.

This test carried more weight for me than it might for most; the past wasn't allowed in the house where I grew up, and I had been raised understanding that I belonged to someone else. I did not have a mother, in the blood and bones sense. So much of my recent family history, beyond my parents and grandparents, was unknown to me, especially on my mother's side, and because she'd died when I was small, I had longed for explanations, or meaning, or any sense of connection for almost as long as I could remember. At the time, I knew nothing about the nascent science behind these tests. I was perplexed by the result but also riveted on many levels. I loved Scandinavia and had only recently heard about the Sámi people, an entire indigenous group with its own language and culture that existed in four countries that were, in part, defined by their homogeneity. I googled the Sámi and was amazed to see pictures of people who looked quite like me – the blonde people, at least, with the same slightly Asian-shaped eyes that had always caused me to wonder what surprises lay in my distant origins. I excitedly emailed friends in Sweden and told them about my discovery. 'This explains why you were so mesmerized by the reindeer at Skansen!' said my friend Henrik, referring to a park in Stockholm where I'd once spent hours watching a herd. 'You must go north!'

For my next vacation, I planned my first visit to the Swedish Arctic, to a small village called Jokkmokk, where a Sámi winter market has been held every February for hundreds of years. In older times, it was a way for people to gather to trade goods and have their children baptized and meet new partners, a respite from the harsh life on the tundra. Now it is also a tourist attraction, with giant Russian women in beaver coats selling wooden spoons and steel-wool pads alongside traditional artisans and their Sámi handicrafts. There are concerts and lectures at the local Sámi museum, Ájtte, and reindeer races. The village buzzes with activity. I am curious about the people, and I instantly love the stark landscapes and the bitter cold, to which I am no stranger, having grown up in Indiana. It is winter that has defined my life.

*

My mother died on 20 January 1975 at 7 a.m. I remember the event, even at three years and four months old, in fine detail in my mind's eye. The softness of the sheets with clouds printed on them, the orange waffle blanket covering us on the king-sized bed, and my mother not waking up as I prodded her to give me a treat from a steel canister that sat by the bed while I snuggled beside her in the crook of her arm.

I know the exact time of her death because my father is a doctor, and because of his training and background, he has always been precise to the point of obsession about details – even in a moment of crisis, even at the moment of the death of his wife and the mother of his four children. Daddy checked my mom's pulse, a sharp intake of breath, and I was scooped up and swiftly carried to my room. I had not met with the idea of death before in any shape or form, and I did not understand what was happening. I only registered on an emotional level that something terrible had taken place when my siblings were called home. Book bags hit the slate floor of the entryway, with screams and tears shortly thereafter. My big sister Anna, who was fourteen at the time and already maternal in her leanings, entered my room and grabbed me, hugging me with all of her might, flush with the fever of hot tears, hyperventilating, her brown hair sticking to her face as she shuddered with sobs. My brothers screamed and slammed doors. It was chaos. Grammie, Mom's mother, arrived, and there were more tears at the sudden and unexpected death of her only child.

Somewhere in another room, my ears pricked up at mention of my name; I heard Grammie discussing arrangements with Daddy as if I could not comprehend that I was being spoken about, the decision that I should not go to the funeral because I was too young and wouldn't understand. It could be traumatic. Everyone grabbed me. Everyone cried harder when they did so. I only know this now as an adult: in the spectrum of grief, there is almost nothing more tragic than a motherless child, except the actual loss of a child. I was bewildered, confused, and I would not understand for some time that my mother had physically left my life forever, and this moment would be the domino from which all others fell, far into my adulthood.

My mother was plagued with a heart problem; my memories are a series of murky vignettes in which I was powerless to save her. On one occasion, she fainted in the hallway and, unable to revive her, I lifted her up, put on my father's giant galoshes and went outside, only to be found by neighbours standing in the street in winter with nothing on but a cloth diaper and undershirt. I remember, another time, we fell off a bike, me in a seat on the back, while going down the steep driveway, leaving us both scraped and bloody, and the peach ice cream that came after the fall. She lost her car keys once at my brother's football game. I don't know why I remember that, other than she was very confused. I had a gold cheerleading outfit and pom-poms that she had made from scratch. Once, I think, I remember her fainting in the bathroom. I could not help.

My mother was a beautiful, creative artist who designed the modern house in which we lived, although she was not an architect. She collected mid-century furniture – Eames chairs and Eero Saarinen dining sets and all manner of bric-a-brac – before it was in vogue. She played the piano. She knew about fashion. She dressed us to the nines. She loved children and crafts and helped start the local version of a Steiner school. She befriended artists and the gay community, not caring what clucking neighbours may have thought in conservative 1970s Indiana. Yet, the only things I can remember first-hand are her suffering and then her exit. It is a constant thought of mine, this: I am filled with deep envy over daughters with mothers. I wish I could tell women who complain about their mothers – I would give anything, almost, to know mine in life, as an adult. To speak to her one time. To know the sound of her voice. How she moved. The colour of her hair. If our hands look the same.

'Did you know you're a bastard?' my best friend and next-door neighbour Richie Beam asked innocently one day as we hung off my swing set in the backyard. I was four years old then, and we were wearing matching red cowboy boots that my dad had got us during a business trip to Texas. I kicked up the dirt.

'What's a bastard?' I asked him.

'You have no mommy.'

But I didn't really think she was gone; I still believed she was just somewhere *else*. Around but somewhere I couldn't see. My father told me, only much later, that I would often climb into the car, whispering into the air-conditioning vents, 'Mom, are you down there?' I asked the teachers and volunteering mothers at my preschool relentlessly if they'd seen her. I regularly checked behind my toy blocks, in closets and in the woods. But she was not there.

My father spent a year doing his best to manage a demanding medical career and raise four kids alone during an era in which men were not expected to do so. I often accompanied him to work at Wishard Memorial Hospital, where he was doing clinical trials on the first synthetic insulin. I spent time with the 'jumpsuit men', the men from the local prison who were doing human trials. They wore orange correctional jumpsuits. They bought me things from the vending machines and told me about their kids. I watched them play pool and watch TV. The nurses and secretaries, most from a combination of genuine compassion and pity for the widowed father and his daughter with the unfortunate bowl cut, gave me candy and pencils and murmured to each other in earshot about how tragic it was that I'd lost my mother. I didn't understand the context, but the feeling – of being singled out, of being pitied, of being talked about – covered me like a grey film that would not wash off. *I am different.*

The memories were too painful at our house, and so Dad quickly sold it and moved us into an apartment. I shared a room with Anna, and my brothers had their own room.

My dad was heroic in trying to manage us all; my life was a patchwork of babysitters and kind women that took me in, before school, after school.

We visited Grammie and Pop Pop, Mom's parents, often – they had moved to Indianapolis from the east coast shortly after I was born – and Grammie took charge of helping us. I found comfort with them; Grammie took me shopping for clothes, made sure my hair was brushed; cooked hearty meals, rubbed my back at night as I fell asleep and sang me the 'Easter Bonnet' song, even when it was December. I watched Lawrence Welk and Don Ho with Pop Pop. I even liked the aroma of Grammie's menthol cigarettes, which she chain-smoked out of nervous energy. The smell calmed me.

And then one day, a year after my mother had died, my father made an announcement to the four of us kids. He was dating. Her name was Joan, and she'd just got her master's in social work. It was very important to my father that I meet her; for some reason I can't understand, I was invited to her house for a sleepover. We visited the Indianapolis Museum of Art – she was also a docent there – and she bought me a butterfly kite. At her house, in an apartment building called the Knoll, we had milkshakes called Alba 77s and watched *Spartacus* on TV. She had white carpet and a blue point Siamese cat named Mousie. Joan was tall and thin with white-blonde hair cut like the ice skater Dorothy Hamill. She had a very large smile. I was tentative towards her – but she swallowed me whole. I went with it.

One month later I was in the car with my dad. I was five years old. He told me that he was going to marry Joan. 'I will always love you, kiddo,' he told me. I wasn't sure what it all meant, but we were all moving in together. They were married in June in Indianapolis. Grammie offered to throw her a shower, but no one came. Pop Pop wrote Dad a long letter, which I only saw for the first time when I was an adult and going through papers. After the wedding Grammie and Pop Pop were moving back to the east coast, to give my father a fresh start with his new wife and family. They wished him the best.

Joan had two daughters, Jane and Linda. They were beautiful. Linda lived in New York and was a journalist. Jane had just graduated from high school and was a student at Indiana University. They did not call Joan mom, or mother, but Joan. I met Linda for the first time at the wedding. She was tall, and thin, and gorgeous. She came with her husband, Chuck. He wore plaid shirts and said the word 'fuck' a lot. His brazenness both shocked and delighted me. I felt as if he was the only person that saw me. He was a foreign correspondent. I was the flower girl, and very nervous. Chuck winked at me as I looked back at him during the ceremony, as if to reassure me. Grammie looked miserable. During the photos with the family, Joan put her bouquet over my face. When the car came to pick up the newlyweds, I asked Joan if I could ride with them in the old-timey car. 'No. This is our wedding,' she said.

Things unravelled for us shortly after Joan arrived. She told my father that she was 'over-stimulated' having two boys in the house. Without explanation, Mark was sent to live in the basement of a minister's house until he was of age to enlist in the military. Anna left, tearfully, for college. I was alone with my brother Will. Sometimes I told stories in the car about my mom; this upset Joan tremendously. My dad came into my room one night and had a chat with me. I couldn't talk about my mom in front of Joan any more. It was too distressing for her.

Joan, who had completed a degree in psychology, decided that Will and I should go to Al-Anon meetings. 'Your mother was a drug addict,' she informed us authoritatively. I was eight years old. 'She was addicted to diet pills. You both need to understand the mind of an addict.' We went to some Al-Anon meetings and got the real-world education of a lifetime. Women talking about their husbands hitting them over the head with frying pans. Broken doors. Broken arms. Gunshots and infidelity. We had never been exposed to things like this. Later, I found out that this wasn't true of my mother at all – it was just something Joan made up in an attempt to justify her hatred of us. But for many years I was left with questions about my mother, and those questions ate at me. They also made me feel damaged, as if I came from a damaged person. Which wasn't true, of course.

Shortly afterwards, Will was sent away to a boarding school in Ohio – at least, that's what I believed was happening at the time. Only much later would I learn that Joan had told him that he was no longer welcome; her psychiatrist had advised that having three adults in the house was too much for her. Will was still in high school. He left, finding work as a cook at a country club one state over and finishing high school alone, away from home and friends.

Then, it was just me and Dad and Joan.

2

ÁILU

I meet Áilu at a wedding. Our eyes lock at the wedding feast – not the recognition of a soul mate or even love at first sight, not nearly, but a profound and foreign feeling I will never forget: *this person is about to play a major role in my life.*

I can feel the piercing stare of his blue eyes from across the crowded wedding hall, past tables and tables of guests in a sea of colourful *gáktis*, the traditional Sámi dress, oceans of blue and red and ribbons and silver.

Kautokeino is not a town that one comes by easily. It is two hours by car from the nearest airport in Alta, a small and pristine city on one of the northernmost fjords in Norway. The Sámi are inhabitants of an area called Sápmi, which encompasses parts of Norway, Sweden, Finland and the Kola Peninsula of Russia and predates the borders of all of these modern countries. I'd spent most of my time on the Swedish side of Sápmi; Norway was not in my mind to visit until I gave a speech at a private gathering in London about my DNA test and growing interest in Sámi culture. An impossibly tall and striking Norwegian man in the audience, Per, introduced himself at the reception and told me he had spent time in the north of Norway with reindeer herders. I did not know much about the Sámi and their interrelationship with majority cultures at the time but understood already that this was unusual. Many Norwegians might go their entire lives without visiting the north, the Sámi culture remaining a mystery. Per, I would learn, was a military veteran and journalist who had ingratiated himself with the working herders enough to travel with them while they were on the *vidda*, the Norwegian word for plateau.

We met for coffee, visited a Lucien Freud exhibition at the National Portrait Gallery and became fast and easy friends; Per felt like a third brother. He immediately introduced me to his good friend Mikko, a former reindeer herder who lived in Karasjok, a village two hours from Kautokeino in the pine forests, surrounded by major reindeer migratory areas. Mikko was a compact man with a shock of blond hair and brilliant blue eyes who talked, smoked and drank a blue streak and wore pointy Cuban heels; he reminded me of a blond version of Simon Cowell. On our first meeting in the summer, arranged by Per, Mikko spirited me around Karasjok, taking me to the old people's home where he was a nurse and introducing me to the local newspaper editor, Stein, who held court in the Karasjok bureau of *Ságat*, the regional Sámi newspaper written in Norwegian. The office was a small red clapboard building with a white picket fence in the centre of town, next to the petrol station and the local pub, Bivdu. The door was open as long as Stein was there, and the cosy building almost invited visitors: it was fashioned much like a house, with a sitting room and kitchen, and locals and travellers from afar streamed through with stories to report, to make complaints or for conversation with Stein, who, when not on deadline, was always ready with a cup of coffee or, at the right hour, some good Spanish red wine.

Coming from a family of journalists and having started my career in the halcyon days of the *Los Angeles Times*, I was enthralled by Stein. He was the quintessential editor of a vintage not often seen in present-day news organizations, which operate impersonally via emails and social media. Stein was fuelled by the stories of others and could listen to people endlessly. Born in the sea Sámi village of Lakselv, an hour away on the coast, he was singular in his understanding of the region and the world beyond, able to discuss almost any topic – international affairs, local Sámi politics (the Norwegian Sámi parliament, the Sámediggi, is conveniently located nearby), conspiracy theories, his days in the Norwegian navy, or the time he lived rough in the pine forests for two months. He also seemed to know the complete biography and history of every reindeer-herding family in Finnmark.

People wanted to tell Stein things. The first time I met Stein on my own, in winter, we made a plan to cross the border to Finland for dinner, thirty minutes away, at a well-worn restaurant and watering hole named Hansa Bar. I walked over to the newspaper office from my hotel and found Stein in deep conversation with a heavily tattooed and pierced teen. I would learn later that he was one of the local Sámi kids caught in the crossfire of Anders Breivik, the Norwegian far-right terrorist who killed sixty-nine kids at a summer camp on the island of Utøya in 2011. The shooting in America at Sandy Hook Elementary School, where twenty-six people, mostly kids, were killed, had taken place that day. Our evening unfolded into an hours-long discussion about gun control. Many foreigners might never fully grasp what a profound impact Utøya had on the hearts and psyches of Norwegians, who lived in a country in which police did not carry guns and a single death might be front-page news for days and reported nationally. And this massacre had hit the north directly: several kids from local villages had been at the camp.

Stein was a person with whom people felt safe, felt heard. He could also drink like he had a wooden leg and had a dry and astute sense of humour – you couldn't help but be drawn to him. Sometimes his stories seemed so outrageous that I'd google them myself later, just to discover they were true. This was Stein.

On a summer visit, we joined Mikko at the local hotel bar, where he spontaneously decided that I needed to come with him to a wedding in Kautokeino, his home-town, the next day. Stein agreed heartily – 'You will never see anything like it in your life' – and encouraged me to go along. And so we drove through pine forests, cutting through the lush greenery and into the open landscape and curving roads dotted with large and rippling lakes, past occasional villages consisting of a few houses, with road signs in Sámi with names I found impossible to pronounce, like *Šuošjávri* and *Láhpoluoppal*. Mikko was giving a lift to two other Sámi men who were also going to the wedding; they sat in the back seat. They spoke no English, and I spoke no Norwegian or Sámi, and so there was silence until a folksy and irrepressibly jingly Norwegian dance-band song by Ole Ivars called 'Karasjok and Kautokeino' came on the radio, and everyone joined in on the refrain with gusto – even the guys in the back, who at that point had started in on Karhu, strong Finnish beer in black cans with a picture of an angry bear on the front, which is how most people who drink the beer end up after several cans.

*

Weddings in Kautokeino are gigantic village-wide affairs, with as many as a thousand guests in attendance at the local community hall. The wedding starts at the church, and then groups begin arriving at the gymnasium, which for every wedding is configured in roughly the same way: rows and rows of tables covered in paper and tea lights, laden with cakes and sweets made by everyone in the village, and at the front of the room, the bride, with heavy silver or gold jewellery on her chest, and groom sitting banquet-style, flanked by their parents. The weddings are community powered, meaning that selected guests, usually friends and family, will take turns serving the *biđus*, a traditional wedding stew made of reindeer meat, potatoes and carrots, alongside buttered bread and *safte*, a watered-down form of soft drink. The *biđus* is cooked in huge vats in a back room, as is the black coffee, of which there is such a volume that it is stirred with a paddle. This part of the wedding may roll on for hours and hours, with people giving up their seats to accommodate the newcomers who wait patiently for their turn to be seated and served. In the evening, a bar is set up, staffed by the men, and the lights are lowered. There is more coffee, and beer, and wine, and music starts – traditional Sámi music called *joik* combined with dance-band and modern music in a mash up of eras and styles. The women do a traditional dance with the bride at the centre, a sort of swaying around in a circle, a bridal symbol of tradition and unity. The night goes on later and later, and eventually an elaborate second meal, a buffet, comes out, banquet tables heaving with piles of smoked salmon and boiled reindeer and breads and salads and cakes. Mikko refers to this as 'night meat', which I find hilarious, although I would come to learn that this was his own English-language invention, and not a translation. The party ends at dawn.

Áilu stays by my side and I joke with him that maybe we could be cousins, a joke that he gets even though his English is halting and I don't remotely speak either of his languages. He is kind. I learn that reindeer are his life. He wants to know everything about New York; he has scarcely been outside of Kautokeino, save for his fifteen minutes of fame when he went to Trondheim in the south for the 1994 Olympics with his reindeer, as part of the televised opening ceremony. If you are a reindeer herder, it is nearly impossible to travel for any length of time because you must always be ready for your herd or making good use of the weather for essential tasks. Globetrotting doesn't fit with the job description.

We spend more time together after the wedding, and when I depart for New York, we communicate daily through Facebook messages whenever Áilu isn't on the mountain, talking about the most mundane details of our days, building a slow and steady friendship, using Google Translate to bridge us when either is at a loss for vocabulary. Our conversations are nothing profound or revealing, just a constant and growing connection that is slowly erasing our greatest commonality: loneliness. In Áilu's world, men are generally partnered and with several kids by his age; family is central in reindeer-herding culture. Áilu has fathered one daughter, Ida, who is fully grown and making her way in the world, and he has never married. The 'bachelor club,' as it is jokingly called in Kautokeino, consists of reindeer-herding men who never managed to settle down or find a partner; they generally live with their mothers until they pass, and then live alone, becoming so set in their ways that they are unlikely to find romantic partners once they reached their fifties, unless they travel to Thailand or the Philippines to find wives, something that happens with increasing frequency in Kautokeino and other Arctic communities. Áilu has simply been so engaged with reindeer herding, and equally so picky, that he has never met anyone with whom to make a life; it was not for lack of women who were interested. But he is very much alone, just as I am alone in New York, an ocean away: meeting a million people a day, never feeling that anyone really knows or understands me.

*

I am terrified to make another mistake in my personal life. I'd met my ex-husband, Richard, through mutual friends on the pretext of possibly working together. He invited me out to lunch several times, on Saturdays, around the corner from my apartment in the Village, at Da Silvano's. We bonded slowly as we both revealed details of our early childhoods; his mother had died at roughly the same age as mine and he had also had a stepmother who resented him deeply. This gave us an emotional connection that couldn't be forged, an unspoken language between us that was already there. Like me, and like so many others that have been dealt unexpected loss and then try to make sense and order out of terrible things, Richard had also spent his life seeking meaning. He was interested in psychology and mysticism and, most of all, art, opening my world to things I'd seen but never remotely understood: de Kooning and Serra and Albers, abstract expressionism and architecture and design. He was a gifted artist, with a collection of art books so extensive that he had to catalogue them. After those Saturday lunches, we would visit museums, pausing for hours at MoMA or PS 31 or in the gardens of the Noguchi Museum in Staten Island. He was a big man, Italian American, with a deep voice and commanding presence. Richard made me feel protected, and he looked after me in a way I'd never known before. He took me shopping and taught me about style and the cut of clothing and designers. He got me books and took me to art shows. No one I'd ever dated had spent money or time or attention on me this way; I was the kid who got clothes from the Value City discount chain in Indianapolis, where there was a sign telling customers not to pee in the dressing rooms.

Soon we were living together on the Lower East Side with plans to marry. 'This is so right that we need to have a child,' Richard said. I was in my middle thirties; we started trying to get pregnant. In my heart, I wanted a child, but I was also terrified of putting another human on earth that might experience what I had and end up abandoned to an unknown fate. The desire for a child lived side by side with fear, filling me with ambivalence in a time that should have been joyous and hopeful. This should have been a warning. For my birthday that year, as a gift, I'd asked to have a lawyer draw up a joint will – before I was even pregnant – stipulating exactly what would happen to our not-even-conceived child if we died. He or she would be raised by one of my best friends, Natalie, the best mother that I knew. No, this wasn't crazy or odd at all.

We married in Italy, outside, on a hotel balcony at the edge of the sea. Just the two of us, no family, no friends. A shadow hung over the day. Something had set Richard off the day before we were to travel south to Capri for the wedding. We were strolling through the Villa Borghese gardens in Rome when he received a phone call, hung up and turned to me. He was angry that I had not returned a call relating to his work – I was also handling his media then. He stood, screaming and yelling, cell phone in hand, as I wept, stunned by the change of mood and level of spitting anger, mortified by the tourists staring at us in horror and curiosity. This was followed by twenty-four hours of stone silence, through Rome and a tour of Hadrian's villa, the temple columns crumbling like my confidence. At breakfast before heading to Capri, I stared into my coffee, feeling sick and wondering whether I should call it all off. But I'd made a commitment, and you just don't abandon people. What I was really facing was my own fear of abandonment: what would I do? And shame: what would people *say*? I remember thinking, *I wish I had a mom to call.*

We were married. We went back to New York. Richard bought an apartment, and in the baby's room of the home he'd lavishly decorated, he ordered a white ten thousand dollar leather couch, just about the last thing that should exist with baby poop and crayons and snot and all the things that come with growing children. We were still trying to get pregnant but couldn't. Richard had the house feng shuied and a Korean shaman acupuncturist come over to give me regular treatments. I found his interest in these things fascinating and charming, until I began to realize these gestures were replacing common sense and simply talking to each other.

There were many people in our life, people who I increasingly sensed weren't real friends, just hangers-on who wanted to be around Richard, who was well known, venerated even, in his field. Crazy hipsters, way too young for either of us to seriously engage with, visited all the time. Richard took them to expensive meals where he'd pontificate. He always paid. I found many of these people vapid and climbing, and it showed in my reactions to them. I had a very high-profile job at that point, and sometimes Richard offered up connections on my behalf without asking. It made me feel used, and I was angry about the inappropriateness.

Nearly a year into our marriage, a giant opportunity presented itself. I was being sent to east Africa for work. I'd dreamed of Africa since I was eleven and writing letters to kids that I'd met through my stepsister, Linda, who was writing a book on the Masai while my brother-in-law, Chuck, was posted in Kenya as the bureau chief of the *LA Times*. I read anything I could on Kenya and devoured Linda's detailed letters home to me describing life there. Joan suggested that I'd be able to visit during a summer break just as Chuck's daughter, Rachel, who was a year older, had done. It was something to look forward to in an otherwise dull Midwestern existence, and I'd spend hours at night in the playground near our house on the swings, flying into the air and fantasizing about meeting my Masai pen pals, William and Joseph, and what I'd bring them (Michael Jackson music and Hershey bars); seeing the cow dung *bomas* in which they lived; riding on Linda's motorcycle through the Rift Valley and meeting her dog, Oomba; and, maybe, visiting the Mount Kenya Club, which I imagined to be lush and fragrant with frangipani and hibiscus and faded diplomats drinking gin and tonics. All of these things sparked my imagination because of the tissue-thin, single-spaced letters typed on green airmail paper that arrived from Linda every few months.

Joan, who'd planted the idea in the first place, but whose moods could also turn on a dime, unceremoniously scuttled the dream of Africa. 'We would never spend that kind of money on you,' she spat one day, and the topic was closed. But Africa still lived in my mind's eye, nearly thirty years later. Professionally, it was a new challenge and I was over the moon about the opportunity.

I was gone for a month, the trip falling during our first anniversary. Richard wrote me a lovely email message acknowledging the day, telling me he loved me and that he and the cats missed me. I had a wonderful trip but was also looking forward to coming home to our new apartment and to resume trying to have a baby.

When I got home, though, Richard was acting strangely. Distant and short. We shared office space and his assistant looked at me guiltily, although I couldn't put my finger on why. Richard was on edge; any small thing would set him off. He thought I'd gained too much weight. And then one night it came, a spear from out of nowhere: 'I think we should get a divorce.'

This took me completely by surprise. Before we'd married, I'd said many times over that, no matter what happened, I never wanted to divorce. Marriage to me meant that we would plough through any problems together, growing in the process and resolving anything that came up. That was the commitment. Otherwise we could just live together.

We spent a couple of months trying to work it out. He revealed that he was extremely irritated that I'd never gone to a self-help retreat he'd suggested in Northern California, which he'd attended several years earlier. I'd never committed because one of the primary conditions of the retreat was no contact with the outside world for seven days, an impossible task for someone leading a small but growing communications consultancy in which clients expected me to be on call and available – that was *the* job. Richard thought I needed to work on myself and would benefit and should go right away. Also, no phones, he reminded me.

The lead-up to leaving for a week and being incommunicado was planned in such detail and secrecy, I can only suppose my clients thought I was going to rehab or that I had terminal cancer. I told Natasha, my close friend and the number two at my firm and the only person who knew where I was going, to call and say someone had died if anything urgent came up. I could not bear to tell people I was so desperate to save my marriage that I was going to a self-help retreat. I flew to Northern California to a place in wine country called the Center. In my 'class' were several Hollywood people, including a well-known screenwriter and an heiress, and an assorted group of others in active emotional distress, with too much money or time, or both. Our phones were whisked away. I spent the next several days in sharing circles listening to what assholes everyone's parents or siblings were and hearing laundry lists of betrayals and grievances running the gamut from Thanksgiving snubs to incest. In one exercise we were given baseball bats and encouraged to beat our rage out on pillows. In another we were driven to a grave-yard, handed a rose and asked to pick a random grave and imagine it was one of our own parents, dead. What would we tell them? On the last day, the head of the retreat, Tim, an unsettlingly charismatic figure, held a birthday party for our 'new selves' and handed out stuffed animals as a token of the work we'd done, supposedly to represent our spirit selves. I got a frog. *That's about right*, I thought.

As I was leaving, Tim patted me on the back. 'I told Richard you did a great job,' he said. It turned out they were friends. I wondered if Richard had been checking on me the entire time.

I got home and went to more marriage counselling, hopeful we'd work it out. But Richard was still acting strangely, as if he were only half there. I returned to the office to find he'd hired a new head of business develop-ment. She had gigantic breasts – I know it's terrible to say that, but it was literally the first thing I noticed – and he couldn't stop talking about her. He refused to introduce us. I was sitting at my desk one day when it hit me out of nowhere: *Richard is having an affair*. I confronted him and he denied it adamantly, but then said he wanted a divorce. I didn't; we'd only been married a year and I did not want the stain of a separation. We were still living together. One morning, Richard had left for work, and I was hurriedly getting ready to go uptown to join a client who was scheduled to appear on a national morning show. I was late. The intercom buzzed; I looked at the security camera and saw a deliveryman with two dozen roses downstairs. I let him in, elated that Richard wanted to reconcile. I knew we would make it.

I opened the door and the man shoved the flowers at me, a giant piece of paper sticking out of them. 'You're served.'

They were divorce papers.

It remains the most spiteful and hurtful thing that anyone has ever done to me.

Three years passed while I threw myself into work, with one disastrous and brief affair in the middle. I was not cut out for the complexity of a relationship.

*

And then there was Áilu. I was drawn to him, and he to me. Our conversations were simple and honest. We were both searching for something we hadn't found in the worlds we inhabited, which couldn't be more different. Maybe this is what makes for a successful relationship, having nothing in common at the start, to be moved purely by feeling rather than intellect. With Áilu there were no neuroses or complicated relationship histories or emotional scars or talk about work. We were both learning completely new worlds, and that seemed enough. On my birthday, he sent me a picture of his gift to me: a reindeer doe, wearing a blue collar with my name written on it. She would live free on the tundra.

Our conversations came frequently and easily. I found safety and comfort in my daily messaging with Áilu, and it was not long before these messages turned into love. He was aware that I was contemplating an extended stay in Karasjok; he also knew that I was moving closer to not wanting to be in New York any more, even though it was impossible to explain to him in detail. He was also intent on leaving his family home; he wanted to settle somewhere else when not on the tundra. He wanted us to live together. 'Come here, Laura,' he wrote one day. 'Don't go to Karasjok. We will be together here.'

3

GUOVDAGEAIDNU

Áilu picks me up in his blue VW van – the reindeer truck I call it – at the train station in Kiruna, Sweden, an Arctic city famous for being the location of the world's largest underground iron ore mine, with a mineral bar so deep and rich that the end has not yet been found or even detected. Every night at 1 a.m. in Kiruna you can feel your bed shake from the nightly dynamite blast forging further into the deposit, down for miles.

The earth underneath the town has been so thoroughly hollowed out that the entire city of Kiruna – historic architecture and all – must now be moved three kilometres away to more solid ground. Kiruna is the closest train stop to Kautokeino, seven hours away by car. I had decided on the train out of necessity: after landing in Stockholm with my cats, Rennie and Boo, I learned that my vet in America had missed a tapeworm treatment for them, required only in Norway, and so I had to decamp to an airport motel in Stockholm for a few days for the mandatory waiting period. The cats were traumatized and meek from the plane ride from New York to Sweden, so when we were ready to travel again, I decided to take the overnight train with them, north through the whole of Sweden, rather than another flight.

Bringing my animals was never in question.

Boo was a rescue cat, adopted from a shelter in Harlem the same day that I saw Richard for the last time. As we sat on a bench in Madison Square Park, the details of the divorce settled, we said our last goodbyes. I had decided that same day to look towards the future and get a companion for my elderly and beloved cat Milo, so I made the trek to Harlem and spotted black and white Boo in a cage, long and lithe and bigger than the other kittens, with a runny nose and eyes. I instinctively knew he was mine the moment I saw him, and the same was the case with Rennie, who was what's known in New York as a colony cat, feral cats who live outside, too wild to become pets, so they're fixed and left to their own devices; you can always tell a colony cat from their chipped ear, indicating they have been spayed or neutered. After being caught for neutering, it was obvious to his rescuers that Rennie wasn't quite tough enough for the streets of New York, so I adopted him one Saturday from the rescue in Union Square, shortly after the passing of Milo.

Boo was a singular feline personality, like Joan Crawford reincarnated: tough and commanding and in charge of his domain, from purring for treats to knocking them off a table with disdain if they weren't the right flavour to glaring at guests of whom he did not approve from his perch on the kitchen bar. Once, Boo let himself out of the apartment while the door was open, stepped on to the open elevator and travelled eight floors down to the lobby for a look around before deciding to return.

Because of his human tendencies, Boo became the subject of photos and memes from the many friends that came to stay at my place when I travelled.

They were my little rocks, Rennie and Boo, the two things that remained the most constant in my world, a universe in which transitions and change were common. And so when I decided to move north, and across an ocean to parts unknown, no matter how temporary that move would be, there was no question that they would come with me on the journey. I knew what it felt like to be abandoned, and I would never do that to my animals.

Áilu boards the train to help me with the cats and my luggage. As he deftly lifts bags, I'm struck once again by his rugged handsomeness. He is not much taller than me – five foot seven at most – with a body strong and lean and compact, with no use for superfluous fat; his body wouldn't know what to do with it. Áilu constantly moves, a bundle of kinetic energy. His face is fine and chiselled, and he is wearing two days of blond beard stubble, hair cut into a short and tidy crop, in direct contrast to his long and unkempt fingernails with visible ridges of dirt underneath, the result of a life spent mostly outside. But what is most striking about Áilu are his eyes: they're the clearest blue, most knowing eyes, and when he stares at you, even in the most mundane of moments, you almost think he is going to tell you the answer to every mystery the universe has ever held, or that he has the power to intuit your deepest secrets, even when he's really only thinking about putting petrol in the van or where he misplaced his knife.

We drive through the lush and verdant Swedish and Finnish Arctic, dense with forest pines and tall grass and blindingly brilliant summer sun that will not abate for twenty-four hours until the solstice. Boo sits on the dashboard, overwhelmed by the world unfolding in front of him. As we cut through Finland and cross into Norway, I have the stacks of paperwork and inoculation information for the cats I have dutifully assembled at the ready, the result of an expenditure of nearly a thousand dollars, multiple vet visits and even a trip to the USDA office next to John F. Kennedy airport to meet the stringent requirements of both taking animals out of the United States and bringing them to Norway. When we arrive at the border, Áilu drives straight through; we aren't even stopped. Partially terrified of breaking a rule, and also wanting to make use of all of the time and money spent on the transit process, I make him turn around and I walk in to the sleepy border office with my thick folders full of veterinary information. 'I have two cats from America,' I tell the border agent, handing him my paperwork. No reaction. He barely looks at it, shrugs his shoulders and waves me on. Just like that.

Kautokeino, or Guovdageaidnu in Sámi, is on the *vidda*, or plateau in Norwegian, making the flora and fauna this high in the Arctic completely different from the areas surrounding it at lower elevations. The land is vast, with sloping hills and great plains dotted with low papery silver birch and loamy tundra, the ground pleasingly soft and spongy because of the lichen, the primary food for reindeer, that covers it. It looks prehistoric, as if this was the way things might have been millions of years ago, when dinosaurs roamed. In the summer, the landscape explodes with colour, made even more vibrant by the contrasts: brilliant blue skies, voluminous and low white clouds, and fields over fields of wildly growing stalks of purple *horbma*, the Sámi word for fireweed, and perky tansy flowers, their perfect yellow buttons saluting the sun. The land is resplendent and alive.

My new home is a town of nearly three thousand people, splayed over the Arctic tundra. Its centre flanks Norwegian National Road E45, a lonely two-lane highway leading to Alta, the nearest major airport, to the north and Finland to the south, the point at which we entered. While there are reindeer owners and herders throughout Sápmi, Kautokeino and Karasjok are the centres of Sámi reindeer-herding culture. As Stein once said, 'It is a culture within a culture,' because there are also forest Sámi, river Sámi and sea Sámi in other areas that have nothing to do with herding. But here, nearly everyone owns or works with reindeer, including Áilu, who left school at thirteen to work full-time as a *boazovázzi*, or reindeer herder. It is a rough, solitary life spent following the changes of nature, with months on the tundra, no vacations and cyclical poverty or wealth, depending on the harshness of the winter and the condition of the herd. Reindeer are sold to slaughterhouses, primarily in fall and midwinter, when they are rounded up from the tundra. In the winter, it's typical to slaughter the reindeer one will use for personal consumption. A very few herders may sell and package their own meat. 'Everywhere I go I am thinking of reindeer,' Áilu told me when we first met. 'Do they have enough food to eat? Are they OK? It is my life.'

Áilu has rented an apartment for us, north of the village centre, next to a gurgling spring on a street called Ájagohpi – three rooms on the ground floor of a creaking blue wooden building with four apartments in total, with an old cast-iron stove, giant picture windows and, thankfully, high-speed Internet. Over my first few days, family and friends visit non-stop: Haettas, Eiras and Gaups, to name a few – there are not many surnames in Sápmi and, it seems, everyone is related. Jet-lagged and overwhelmed, I make a chart, discreetly taped to the back of the bedroom door, to get the names straight. First names are also from a limited pool in large part: Inger, Risten and Berit, Johan and Nils, for example, further complicated by the same middle names in various combinations. There are no knocks on the door: visitors just appear out of nowhere. My lack of Norwegian or Sámi and their lack of English is no barrier. At first, I believe it is just curiosity driving the visitors to us – the crazy woman who has come halfway around the world, from New York City, with two cats, to live in this Arctic village. But I am wrong: this is commonplace and my cultural notions of the art of receiving guests are irrelevant here. This is how visitors come, randomly and without notice, and it is completely different from New York, where visits need to be scheduled out of respect for personal space.

Áilu has never lived outside of his family home – basically a depot for his time not spent in the mountains and following the reindeer – and clearly he has been resourceful in outfitting his first independent home, our 1970s-era apartment, with furniture from the same period assembled from a variety of sources: an ancient drum washer in the bathroom lent by a sister-in-law; a tatty black sofa set from another reindeer-herding brother; some old worn twin beds from his parents' house; a chair from his sister; and a big 1980s TV. The apartment is basic and

its contents, a jumble of mismatched and worn familial donations, an eyesore even, but there is something
exceedingly touching about Áilu's dedication to trying to
create a home.

I unpack my clothing and find a box for litter, and I'm
grateful to learn there are two grocery stores in town, both
of which sell cat litter and cat food, a concern I'd had earlier
because it is dogs, not cats, that are primarily owned by
herders. Kautokeino is a town with services, of course – a
hotel, two petrol stations and the Sámi University College,
the local university, but even though I had talked to Áilu
previously about the town, and been at the wedding the
year before, I had had no chance to explore, and I held the
village in my mind's eye as being devoid of the places and
everyday utilities that make a community run, particularly
because so much of my pre-arrival experience had been
based on hearing Áilu describe his activities as a herder,
which rarely included spending time in the village, aside
from visiting his sisters for coffee or stopping into the
Rema 1000 market for butter. His shopping trips were
mostly relegated to when he needed to supplement food
for the reindeer – purchased in nearby Finland – when he
wasn't cutting firewood, mending fences or travelling out
to monitor the herd.

We have three sets of neighbours, one on top and two
to our left, but despite Áilu's friends dropping by, no one
in our building seems to be coming around with a Bundt
cake and a warm welcome, which surprises me, because
it is such a contrast to our other visitors – but then again,
those were all people Áilu knew. A couple of times I see
our next-door neighbours on the ground floor, because
we share a small entryway. Each time the woman sees me

she looks at me suspiciously and doesn't say hello; when the door to their apartment opens I'm overwhelmed by the stench of cigarettes and boiled reindeer meat and fat that permeates the foyer. If we happen to be leaving, she often asks Áilu for a ride, and he always says no, curtly explaining to me that it's 'better not to get involved, or I will be driving all the time'. I see a man go into the apartment occasionally, or walking outside, eyes glazed over in a drunken stupor.

*

By the start of August, what is left of the summer, as is the case with every season in the Arctic, is spent diligently preparing for the season that will follow. Áilu mends fences endlessly, fixes his snowmobiles, chops firewood and does small jobs for the local village kommune to earn extra cash. I start to fix up the apartment and spend what feels like hours over hours hanging sheets from the drum washer outside to dry; I am still hilariously oblivious to the fact that people do have normal state-of-the-art washing machines in their houses here – our washer is purely a function of Áilu's economy. I start to learn how to drive an ATV, and in our off time, we frequently visit the homes of Áilu's three sisters, Sofe, Risten and Rávdná. Sofe and Risten work in the local schools as teachers and administrators, and Rávdná works in a hospital as a nurse and is married to a traditional reindeer herder. She has started a reindeer meat shop in a building adjacent to their house. We drink coffee at their homes and visit for hours; all speak perfect English and are eager to teach me about Sámi culture and language. We go fishing one afternoon with the families, and I am amazed to see Áilu's sister-in-law Lejá Karin, a beautiful blonde, manoeuvre an ATV over a perilous terrain of rocks while holding a baby and an additional toddler in front of her.

'How are you doing that?' I marvel out loud.

She laughs. 'Laura, I have done this since a child – it's our way!'

Every reindeer herder's family has a summer and a winter place. Áilu's family's summer place is in Ruddojávri, an hour away from Kautokeino by car and then another two hours over the hilly tundra by ATV. We go to check the cabin, as well as to relax. We take Áilu's reindeer-herding dog, Čáhppe, who has been otherwise relegated to his parents' house out of fear that he will maul Rennie and Boo. A Lapponian herder, or Sámi reindeer-herding dog, Čáhppe has been born and bred to work; he runs single-mindedly kilometre after kilometre after the ATV, over the verdant hills, stopping only occasionally to slurp water from puddles, seemingly incapable of exhaustion. As an animal lover, I adore Čáhppe from the start and feel a terrible guilt that he's been banished because of my cats. I often feed him treats like dried pig ears or hot-dogs from the petrol station, which he gobbles up summarily. Finally Áilu, in the gentlest of ways, explains to me that I need to stop feeding his dog. Čáhppe is a working dog. 'You are softening Čáhppe,' he explains. 'He is my partner in work. When I eat, he eats. If we run out of food on the mountain, he must be able to continue. You cannot spoil him all the time – it doesn't help.' This fundamental difference in how animals are regarded is one of the major differences between us from the start, and the disparate thinking grows the longer I stay. Áilu and many others are both amused and perplexed by my bringing my cats across an ocean, as well as how I respond to the herding dogs when I see them – cooing and petting them as if they were children. To me, animals are pets, friends and companions. To Áilu, animals are partners in survival, to be respected and taken care of, but not treated in a frivolous manner. Even the animals must be tough on the tundra. I imagine more than once that Áilu might literally die of shock if he ever saw Petco, the giant pet store near my old apartment in Union Square in New York, occupying one half of a city block and filled with aisle over aisle of squeaky toys and dog shampoos and clothing and reindeer antlers sold as dog chews for ten dollars.

Like most traditional *hytta* – the Norwegian word for a cabin – Áilu's family's is simple and austere. There is no running water; it is collected in jugs from the enormous shallow lake just outside. Electricity is run from a battery when necessary, mostly for cell phones, and there is a giant, ancient cast-iron and white-enamel oven that must be stoked through the burners for heat and cooking. The beds are covered with generations of worn blankets and clothing from all of the children and grandchildren that have passed through.

Áilu keeps a handwritten count of the reindeer owed to him by others hidden on the back of a cracked mirror that hangs in the living room. We eat dried reindeer meat cut and served with hard butter, using an outdoor knife. These are Áilu's primary food sources and all I ever see him eating, along with gallons of thin black coffee. There isn't an ounce of fat on Áilu's body – he is all muscle and sinew – and more than once I imagine a scenario in which some crazy entrepreneur stumbles on this way of eating, which is Áilu's own, and invents the 'Sámi reindeer diet'.

In the afternoons we push the boat out on the bracing Arctic lake water and row, the lake bottom too rocky to swim. We practise shooting with an old rifle, and I learn how to manoeuvre the ATV straight up steep hills, nearly flipping the heavy machine, narrowly avoiding breaking both of our necks in the process. Other than the noises we have brought, the world is totally silent, vast and pristine. I feel the shell of city life slowly, slowly beginning to crack and loosen, giving way to the smallest glimmer of wonder and possibility, things that have been missing from my life longer than I had realized, until now. I have no control over my anxiety here because I have no control in general; this place is utterly unknown to me and I am reliant on others – Áilu, primarily – to show me and teach me and guide me. There is nothing to worry about because I simply do not know *what* to worry about; my anxiety has no frame or anchor and so it wanders elsewhere for the moment.

This total loss of control feels liberating and foreign, as if I can breathe for the first time. There is space. There is something else, as well: the invigorating feeling that everything is new here and unknown, and with the unknown comes a hopeful feeling. There had been so many disappointments before I'd left, I'd wondered if I'd ever have this feeling again. There is a sense of honest possibility, of not knowing what the next day might hold and being excited to wake up and see what new experience awaits or what I need to learn or do. It is the night-before-Christmas feeling in an adult existence. And none of these things involve money or stature: they involve being in the moment and relinquishing control. When I left New York, I was exhausted – emotionally, financially and physically, as if I had been on a giant rat wheel from which there would be no end. And it was easy to stay on the rat wheel and become oblivious and anaesthetized, dying a little every day – in my case, numbed by booze and Netflix bingeing and psychoanalysing, self-pity and shame. Being introspective felt like an indulgence I did not deserve, and I knew a more enlightened person would have managed better. I shied away from yoga and meditation and ideas like 'self-care' – I even had contempt for these practices, as I had encountered them long after they had morphed from their original concepts into the province of the disproportionately wealthy businesspeople who were part of my culture and work world, people singularly focused on optimizing every experience for the maximum outcome and then bragging about it on social media.

Thankfully, I am now a million miles away from anyone that understands 'life hacks' and people who drink grass-fed yak-butter coffee or do six-day silent meditation retreats in exotic locales and then write extensive posts about their personal growth on LinkedIn and Instagram with hashtags like #blessed. It was, to me, unsustainable and disingenuous and, most of all, exhausting. I couldn't keep up, and I hated it. I had started to feel terrible about myself all the time. Now it is simple. There is no noise and no distraction. I have to be with myself, whatever that means, in the silence, listening to nature, being still.

*

Summer switches into autumn almost overnight. The fire-weed, once green and purple, are now gold and red, their fuzzy white spores, like particles of down pillow filling, blowing in the breeze. Change is afoot, from the land to the sky, and you can feel it in the crisp air and the rustling of the silver birch leaves and the rimy frost that starts to form on the windowsills in the mornings. I am starting to settle in, although after three months, communicating with others through hand gestures and nods for more complicated conversations has become exhausting for all involved. I can tell that having to search for words in an effort to include me is tiring for those that speak some English. It's clear that I need to learn the Sámi language, the primary language of Áilu's family and this part of the north. On one of my first visits I was astounded to learn that Norway has two official languages, Norwegian and Sámi – although if you started to speak Sámi in any major city in Norway, or even at a restaurant in nearby Alta, you'd likely be met with blank stares. There are only about forty thousand speakers of Sámi language in Norway, but it is essential to understanding the culture.

Speaking Sámi was forbidden, treated as shameful and a point of ostracization, from the 1800s until the 1980s, and Sámi children were taken from their homes and sent to boarding schools to learn and speak Norwegian in a policy of forced assimilation known as Norweginzation. There are generations who know Sámi as the language spoken at home and in whispers, but who never learned to read or write it formally. Since that time, the Sámi language in Norway has started to experience a powerful renaissance, in part because of Norway's support of its revitalization as an act of contrition for its brutal past policies. As an official language of Norway, there now are Sámi language news channels and radio stations; if you drive in the streets in the north, or visit the shops, you will see signs in Sámi along with their Norwegian counterparts. It is the operating language of my village, the language Áilu and his family speak, the language of reindeer herding and of my neighbours. It is also the language that unlocks the secrets of where I reside: every street name, every place name contains more than the name itself, says something essential about its state. Ájagohpi, the street on which I live, is named after a spring, or *ája*, while *gohpi* is a pit – and that spring trickles from the sloping hill just like water trickling down into a pit. Even the village name, Kautokeino (Guovdageaidnu), means middle place, between reindeer-herding areas. To know the language is to understand the deeper meaning of this part of Sápmi.

I have always found language-learning challenging – dismal at unfamiliar pronunciations, my brain mixing words and phrases into jumbles. While studying French in college, I passed my language requirement, not for my prowess in coherently discussing *L'Etranger*, but for giving the ancient French teacher rides home every week. Here I cannot survive on smiles and nods forever. This will be my most difficult challenge yet – Sámi is a Uralic language, with a totally different structure from English or Romance languages, like nothing I've ever encountered and no ready framework for my brain to grasp. But I must learn, or at least try.

I enrol at the local university for an intense semester-long beginner-level immersion course that's held in two parts. We must only speak in Sámi – mother tongue or speaking of one's native majority language is totally forbidden. The Sámi language books are taught through Swedish, Finnish and Norwegian. This presents a major problem that will lead to some hilarious misunderstandings as I move forward. To start, I speak none of these languages, adding an extra layer of translation and frustration. But the people who have joined my beginner class fascinate me. There are Åsa and Josephine, young and ambitious Swedish Sámi women eager to further Sámi rights through their jobs in Sámi government, and three later-middle-aged Russian Sámis who saved everything to come to Norway to study for a brief period – no place in Sápmi has been more restrictive and less acknowledging of Sámi culture than Russia, and so they are eager to learn and take knowledge back home to their kids and grandchildren. Even though the dialect of Sámi in their region, Kildin Sámi, is entirely different, this is a start, a taste. There are three young students on an exchange programme from Yakutia, a place known for diamonds, horses and some of the coldest temperatures on earth – it is also the home of the Kingdom of Permafrost tourist attraction.

My first friend among the Russians is the fifty-something Vadim, who drives an ancient white Russian Lada pockmarked with scars of rust and gives us all rides to class in the morning in the frigid cold, his car choking up the main hill that cuts across Kautokeino. I pay Vadim in cabbage and a single can of beer on a couple of Fridays, a way of saying thank you; with no shared language, we have no other way to communicate save for our actions and smiles and sympathetic clucks. When I walk by the windows of the student housing in the evenings, I see

Vadim in the window playing his guitar and imagine what he gave up to come here.

Another friend is Eva, the beautiful professional Swedish hunter and dog trainer who grew up in Swedish Sápmi, an actual survivalist, not of the ilk found on reality television. Eva travels everywhere with her hunting dog, a beautiful male pointer named Min. At times I see her biting so hard on her pencil as she studies that I wonder if a tooth will come out. She is learning Sámi because her father, a well-known hunter who had since died, was friends with many Sámis, and now she is with a Sámi reindeer herder in Sweden, often working with him and the herd. She is kind and determined and laughs uproariously at everything I say, which makes me like her even more.

My closest friend in school, however, is Yoko, a Japanese student taking a break from her sociology PhD work in Tromsø to live in Kautokeino for a semester and dive into the culture. Like me, she is totally out of her element, but she has a wonderful childlike quality and an infectious enthusiasm. Yoko's second language is English but she speaks it perfectly. She is as lost as I am in the class because we don't understand any of the languages of instruction in the textbooks. Also, in Sámi, conjugations are completely different from those in English and Romance languages, and understanding this essential architecture is vital. Amazingly, we do have one small tool: nearly a decade earlier, a Japanese scholar named Kingo Yoshida had come to Sápmi and written a small primer in Japanese on how the Sámi language is structured. Yoko has this book, and I sit huddled next to her asking her to translate key ideas from Japanese into English.

The teachers deeply believe in the immersion method and we are sternly admonished every time we whisper to each other in English. While well-intentioned, the problem with this method of teaching is that you can say the word *banana* five hundred times in Sámi, but until there is a picture of a banana in front of you, you won't get it. We do our best to keep up: we write out our oral assignments phonetically and I ask endless questions of Áilu's sisters. Yoko and I can't help but laugh when we realize it has taken the two of us hours to get through one simple assignment: explaining in Sámi language a simple Sámi children's picture book called *Naggaris Emma*, about an annoying six-year-old girl who won't do as she's told. This book would come to be my *War and Peace*. At night I go home, brain exploding, cranky and exhausted, putting further wear on Áilu, who is forced to put his reindeer-herding man-of-the-tundra persona aside and try to explain to me why Emma won't take a bath. It feels like an uphill battle.

The best part of the class is when we have immersion assignments outside of the classroom, going to different places in the village to put our language into action. The first one I have is to go to the *mánáidgárdi* directly across from our house. This is the Sámi word for what is known in Norwegian as a *barnehage*, a kindergarten or daycare for kids between the ages of one and five. I bring my assignment – to learn words related to the school – and am immediately greeted by a gaggle of children, a couple of whom speak Sámi, Norwegian and English, thanks to television. A precocious five-year-old, remarkably also named Emma, like the girl in the book, grabs my work-sheet, reviews it authoritatively and pulls out a picture book. 'Listen to me. I'm the teacher. Sit down.' I stumble on some words she's showing me. 'Laura, you say that wrong. You need to try again,' she admonishes me. I don't know whether to laugh or to cry.

Another day we are sent as a class to the Arbeidssenter, a work centre in the middle of the village for people with disabilities and other vocational challenges, who are not traditionally employable. The people at the Arbeidssenter make handicrafts for sale, host coffees for the older people in the village, do laundry, cut, package and sell firewood, and run a second-hand shop, among other things. We are put on rotation to learn various tasks and the associated words; I stir and cook *biđus*, Sámi reindeer stew, in the kitchen, learning the words for pot and spoon and cooking and meat. Then I am sent to the basement to learn cleaning words, where I am paired with my next-door neighbour, who is called Solla. She hands me a bucket and mop, tells me to clean the floor and then leaves. I can think of nothing else other than the fact that I understood her, and I feel triumphant.

4

DETRITUS

After my brother Will was sent away, I was alone
with Dad and Joan. We'd moved to a secluded
suburb of Indianapolis. We lived in a long ranch
house, built in the 1950s, with a cul-de-sac driveway and
'wings' of the house sectioned off by a foyer with glass
windows. My bedroom was on one side of the house and
Dad and Joan's on the other. The house was in the woods,
and I often got scared at night when branches scraped
the window or the wind blew particularly hard. As any
child from the Midwest will tell you, the woods can be
a scary place where runaway murderers from the state
penitentiary might be hiding, or ghosts, or red-eyed
demons ready to snatch souls.

When I'd become particularly scared, I would steel
myself to make the run across the glass-windowed foyer
and past the family room to the other side of the house
to wake my father up and get him to sleep in one of my
twin beds until I could fall asleep. Joan found this inappropriate and told me that I couldn't come get my dad in
the night any more, and I was not allowed to go in their
room. I still got scared, so instead I hid in the laundry

basket in a closet opposite their bedroom, trying to get up and back to my own bed in the morning before I was found. I could hear my dad snoring through the wall and it made me feel safer. I slept there or in the windowless furnace room, in the centre of the house, under my dad's old army blanket from Korea and with some of my dolls.

Our entire family, and all of the kids in our blended family, never came together again after the wedding. With Will in boarding school, Mark in the military, Linda overseas and Anna in college, I was on my own. I didn't know or understand why, but no one even came home for Christmas, or Thanksgiving, or other holidays in the way that a normal Midwestern family – meaning practically everyone else – did. It was as if I was an only child, unless Jane and her boyfriend, with whom she now lived nearby, visited, or Anna drove down from a town called Terre Haute, where her college was located, and took me to the mall. Anna was still maternal and also funny; she blasted Elton John, her absolute favourite person on earth, and started 'Rocket Man' singalongs in the car. She bought me blue plastic new-wave sunglasses and we took black and white photos in the shopping mall photo booth, sticking out our tongues and crossing our eyes. Wherever Anna went, she helped everyone she saw, from old ladies crossing streets, to kids who'd become lost, to the grumpy clerk at the pretzel place in the mall who lost her keys. It was as if she could feel what people needed and brought light in even the most mundane situations. She was the kindest person I'd ever met, and she felt more like a second mother than a sister to me; she was the one that held me after my mother died, sat with me when I had the flu and it was 'coming out of both ends', as she would hilariously put it, sewed me outfits in home economics and took me everywhere. I missed her when she was away.

In some ways, life was predictable, routine and perfectly Midwestern. Every Saturday, without fail, I would watch cartoons and have waffles and then go on errands with my dad: the hardware store, Radio Shack, the electronics store, the liquor store, the drugstore and the dry-cleaners, followed by a scoop of mint chocolate chip ice cream at Baskin Robbins. Saturday nights, Dad and Joan would go on their 'Saturday night date', which was adults only, and I would stay home with a babysitter and eat Hungry-Man TV dinners and watch *Love Boat* and *Fantasy Island* and *Saturday Night Live* and *The Benny Hill Show*, the last programme before the TV stations played the national anthem and then signed off to white noise and fuzz. Sundays we would go to Presbyterian church and lunch at the country club.

Out of the blue, Joan decided to adopt me as her own daughter. To me, this was thrilling; I wanted nothing more than to have a mother, and I craved Joan's attention and love and acceptance; she seemed to vacillate between dominating me, reminding me that I was hers, and telling me she was not my mother, letting me know that I was the product of a troubled person and the manipulative Galloways – my siblings. I never knew what I was going to get from day to day and believed the adoption would make me safe – she would formally be my mother, at least. I would be hers and I wouldn't go away like the other Galloway kids. The idea also seemed to thrill my father, as there was always a sadness hovering in the background. I wanted his approval, too.

Social workers came to the house and interviewed me. They held clipboards and looked at my bedroom and asked me about school and ballet lessons, just like in the movies. I went with Dad and Joan to the courthouse in downtown Indianapolis and I stood before a judge who approved the adoption and told me I was a fine young girl and best of luck in my future. My birth certificate was replaced. There was now no record of my mother, Shirlee Delpiaz Galloway. She was replaced by Joan.

Joan and my dad travelled a lot, around the world, for my father's work and on vacations. I stayed with neighbours and babysitters. Despite the fact that she was mercurial, there were things that I really loved about Joan. She always brought back presents from their trips – dolls and hotel soaps. I was hungry to learn and we watched the *The Today Show* nearly every morning. She was very cultured and I learned about things like Courrèges purses from France and art history. We went to lectures at the local library, and she let me take the bus downtown by myself. We had chicken salad lunches in an Indianapolis landmark, the Ayres tearoom, and we watched and discussed Phil Donahue, an American talk-show host. Joan also started to confide in me the way that an adult might confide in another adult. She told me that I didn't understand what she had to put up with with my father and my brothers. She and Dad argued a lot about my brothers and I didn't know why. She began to talk to me about leaving my dad, and saying that now she had adopted me I was her daughter, and we could go together and start a new life. I loved my father so much, and he was always good to me, so I was confused about who the bad guy was in the situation. I couldn't imagine leaving my father, but maybe he was terrible. I just didn't know. And I wanted Joan to love me, possibly more than anything I'd ever wanted in my life.

One night they had a fight – Joan is not a drinker by any stretch, but she'd had a couple of gin and tonics and was in a rage. Then she had a Valium because she was 'over-stimulated' and crying and screaming at my father, telling him to leave, just get out. She called him a prick. 'Get out of our house, you prick!' I was afraid, and I parroted her, yelling the same words at my dad. 'Get out of the house, you fucking prick!' He got his keys and went, silently. I put Joan in her nightgown, wiped her nose and got her to bed, and when she fell asleep I got on my bike and spent the night in a cluster of pine trees next to our house. It just felt safer there.

The fight passed. One day Anna called us to tell us she was getting married to a guy from a deeply religious coal-mining family. He was an engineer. I hadn't seen my brothers for years, but they both came for the wedding in rural Indiana. I couldn't stop looking at Mark and how he'd changed; the last time I'd seen him I was eight, and now I was fourteen. He'd completely grown up and was an adult now, and I didn't even recognize him. Grammie and Pop Pop were also there, and it was very tense. I hadn't seen them for years, either, but always got cards with money in them at Christmas, Easter and my birthday. My own blood relatives felt strange to me, and I sensed that my siblings felt I was part of another family now, in which they were not included, with my dad and Joan. I felt guilty, as if I'd betrayed them by getting adopted. I didn't really belong to them any more, and I didn't entirely belong to Joan – she reminded me frequently that I was not her blood daughter and that Jane and Linda were. When people asked her how many kids she had, she said two. She told me that I'd have to watch my weight because my mother was heavy, and I didn't have Joan's genes.

While Linda was in Africa, she and Joan often wrote to each other. Joan wrote from her office room, which was in the same part of the house as my room and Will's former bedroom. It had gold carpet and an Asian-style desk with her typewriter on top. I was utterly terrified to enter this room, somehow believing that Joan would know that I was there, even if I didn't touch anything. I heard Joan typing mostly on the weekends, responding to one of Linda's letters. They seemed to have a love–hate relationship – once when Linda had come the thirteen thousand kilometres from Africa to Indiana on a visit, Joan had thrown her out over a disagreement, telling her to go back to Africa. I never knew what Joan was writing in her letters until one day I crept in to her office, my fear of being caught eclipsed by overwhelming curiosity. I just remember one thing from the letter laid out on her desk – seeing my name beside the word *detritus*, which I then had to look up in my dad's giant dictionary that always lay open on a stand in his office. The sentence read: 'Laura is the detritus of her father's life with a slut.'

I was in junior high when my father started to take me out of school, on the pretext of orthodontist appointments, to have meetings at Dalt's, a local restaurant, to talk about Joan. My dad told me that Joan had problems that probably stemmed from childhood, and she was deeply jealous of us kids. Dad was seeing a psychiatrist almost weekly then, and told me that Joan felt threatened by the Galloways and asked if I wanted to talk about it.

Joan told me frequently that I was a master manipulator and she couldn't stand it. Because I was a Galloway and part of the problem, I'd started trying to be perfect: if I practised gymnastics and didn't do a perfect somersault or headstand, I had to repeat it fifty times, head aching, until I reached perfection. My things in my bedroom had to be in detailed order before I went to bed, with all shoes unlaced and lined up, closet hangers pointing in the right direction, closet doors closed. If I made a mistake and left a crease on my made bed, I believed I would be punished with bad luck. I worried about fires and had to check the burners on the hob several times before leaving home, lest I caused an accident. I washed my hands constantly. No one saw me doing those things. I was also very afraid of going to hell and that I was a bad person, because I had learned in church that Jesus died for my sins and I felt terrible that I caused someone to die. The guilt overwhelmed me and I prayed constantly for forgiveness.

I didn't tell my father any of this for fear of having him think that I was somehow broken or defective, proving everything Joan thought about the Galloways true. Instead, at Dalt's, I apologize to my dad for having called him a prick; this ate at me constantly as one of the worst things I'd ever done. 'It's OK, honey,' he said. 'You were just protecting yourself.'

Things were so unstable at home, and because Joan clearly didn't want me in the house, I was terrified of being thrown out at any moment. I had asked the youth minister at our church if there were any old people with whom I could live and do work in exchange for room and board, but there was no one. I shared this idea with my dad and he told me at Dalt's that he would understand if I left, that I was in a very unhealthy environment. He was sympathetic and loving, and said I should go if I thought that's what was best for me. It didn't escape me that he didn't want me to stay.

Anna was now living in Rhode Island, newly married and working in real estate, trying to get pregnant – the only thing she had ever wanted was to be a mother. She was part of her husband's family now and spent holidays with them; they were tight-knit people who welcomed her into their fold. I didn't see her often, but she sent me hilarious postcards from a seagull that visited her yard who she called Merlin.

*

I felt joyful every year when school ended; this was because every summer from the time I was eight years old I was sent to camp for several weeks. The camp was exclusively for girls and was called Rockbrook, in the Blue Ridge mountains in North Carolina. It was very genteel, filled with well-heeled southern girls. We wore uniforms on Sunday and learned to ride and shoot. I loved it because the counsellors were kind and atten-tive, and it was like being in a family. I thrived there; without trying, I forgot things that I needed to worry about at home. I felt like I belonged. People wanted to be around me and I made friends and laughed and didn't have time to think about turning off the burners on the hob or Jesus dying for my sins or 'overstimulating' Joan or being told that I needed to watch it because I was a little manipulator. I loved the camp until I was fifteen, the summer that I believed I was in love for the first time and too old to go. I wrote Joan a heartfelt letter asking not to be sent away and brought it to her one morning, folded up, along with her coffee and the morning newspaper, and anxiously awaited her response. I was hoping for a good outcome because letter writing worked for my best friend Stephanie when she was grounded and wanted to go to a Billy Idol concert. She just told her mother how much it meant to her. Joan came into my room glaring, letter in hand. 'Who the hell do you think you are?' she asked me. I went to camp.

I was miserable in North Carolina. Joan had instructed the camp administrators not to allow me to make any calls home, which made me feel even more isolated. No amount of fried chicken or sweet tea or bonfires and mountain air could make me feel at ease. One day I sneaked a phone call to Anna from a pay phone and she considered – in all seriousness – coming to get me and letting me live with her. She'd seen my brothers struggling in the world with no place to go and she didn't want to leave me behind. We decided against this plan when Anna figured out that, even though she was my older sister, it would be kidnapping. I talked to Teed, who ran the camp and had known me since I had pigtails and two giant front teeth. Teed was a steel magnolia, used to dealing with parents and, having run a camp for thirty years, knew about kids and when something was really a problem to be tackled or when it was just whining. I didn't know what Teed said to my parents or how she persuaded them, but one day a ticket back to Indiana arrived out of the blue, mid camp session.

I got off the plane and Joan welcomed me home as if nothing had happened. There were even flowers in my room. I could stay home for the summer under two conditions: that I get a job and learn to drive. There weren't many work options for a fifteen-year-old girl who couldn't drive, but thankfully, we were now living in a condo community near which, a mere ten-minute bike ride away, was a strip mall containing a dry cleaner's, a Barney's chain restaurant and a Supercuts hair salon. The Supercuts was hiring for a receptionist and the job would be to sweep hair, manage the receptionist desk at the front and run the cash register. I interviewed with a tiny woman with brown hair who managed the store, called Carol. She was very businesslike when she interviewed me – lateness would not be tolerated. I got the job.

I was very excited about my new job at Supercuts. We were supposed to wear white or blue pants and I was given a Supercuts smock to wear with the company logo on it. I stood at the receptionist desk and wrote haircut orders down on tickets – mostly men getting clipper cuts but also thrifty women getting new hairstyles. I had to clean the combs and clippers in blue tubs of Barbicide disinfectant out the back in between taking orders and sweeping hair. The day was filled with small talk and chatter – how's the weather and so on – between the customers and the hairstylists. It was hard work; everyone was on their feet all day, and the hair cutters' performance was based on how many customers they could process in an hour. It was minimum wage, plus tips.

Carol was a taskmaster and very goal oriented; she ran a tight ship and didn't seem to like me much, for no apparent reason. Kristy, who chain-smoked Kool cigarettes during breaks in the back room, barely gave me the time of day and was quick to snap if I recorded a haircut in the wrong way or didn't stamp my time card correctly. One day I overheard Becky, one of the stylists, calling me 'rich bitch' behind my back in the break room and everyone laughed. People knew that I came from privilege, that my father was a doctor and I lived in an upscale community nearby. I suppose they thought I didn't 'need' the job. I started to dread coming in to work, knowing I was being talked about and that I wasn't part of the club. If only they knew.

One early autumn Saturday, the reception area was packed with customers, mostly men, waiting to get their haircuts. As I stood at the register, I saw Joan driving up in her Mercedes, seemingly in a rage. The front door of the shop flew open and Joan glared at me and yelled, in the middle of the packed reception area, 'You fucking whore! Are you pregnant? *Are you pregnant?*' Carol dropped the comb she was holding. Everything stopped. Jaws dropped. Customers looked at me, eyes wide, agog. I was stunned; I had absolutely no idea what was happening. *At all.* Joan held a brown paper bag in her hand.

'Ma'am, why don't you take this into the back room?' Carol said calmly. She unlocked the manager's office and I learned that Joan had gone through the trash in my bedroom. A week earlier, after a sex education class in school, I'd taken the bus downtown with my best friend Stephanie to visit Planned Parenthood. I'd been given the pill. I was a virgin and hadn't intended to have sex; it was really more the thrill of feeling grown up. When I came home, I'd thrown the bag and the receipt in the trash in my room, not thinking twice about it. Until now.

I reassured Joan that I was not pregnant and had never had sex. Joan unleashed a tirade and left. I was terrified: of being thrown out, of being sent away – and for something I didn't do.

'Well, that was something,' Carol said calmly. 'Honey, would you like to clock out and take a break? I can't imagine anyone talking to their child like that.' She touched my hand gently in an act of reassurance. Kristy even hugged me.

*

Earlier that year, during spring, there'd been a joyous arrival: after two years of trying, Anna had had her first child. It was all she'd ever wanted and she was thrilled; she immediately started sending us funny pictures of my new nephew dressed up in his baby outfits, sleeping in his crib, eating and with his stuffed animals. I loved to look at pictures of him, to see if he looked like us and whom he looked like most. I loved to say that he was ours – he was a Galloway. He was born to a person whose singular wish was to have a baby, and I could think of no better mother than Anna. She held us together when our own mother died.

The baby was about five months old when Anna called my dad from Rhode Island to say that her back had been hurting terribly and she had a fever. My dad assured her that it was likely nothing and urged her to see her doctor; he said he'd make an appointment at Rhode Island hospital if needed.

Anna called back with terrible and unexpected news. She had advanced leukaemia. It was August. She was admitted to the hospital for treatment and we spoke only once, an uncomfortable silence hanging over the phone call because I didn't know what to say or ask. Anna did. 'Laura, I've lost all of my hair and look like Kojak.' She laughed. She had cancer and was putting me at ease. This was Anna.

It seemed the chemotherapy was working and Anna was sent home for a bit. We were all hopeful. And then a few weeks later, the day before my sixteenth birthday, Anna was readmitted to the hospital. My dad flew out to Rhode Island to be near her, and I asked to go with him, but Joan said no because I would get in the way. I couldn't concentrate at school – all I could do was think about her. I knew she was going to be OK, though – I had to believe this. Our family had already paid our dues in the loss department with Mom dying and all of us being separated. Anna had a new baby, and she was only twenty-seven years old. No, she wouldn't die. I thought about this as we studied Chaucer in English class and my mind drifted endlessly. I reasoned with God and tried to pray to anyone that might listen.

A few nights later, I had an extremely vivid dream. Anna was sitting with me, joking around. She was wearing a pink angora sweater and her hair was thick and shiny, in a cascade of long chestnut curls. Her cheeks were rosy, and she almost glowed. She was happy and bright and she took my hand. 'Everything is OK,' she told me. 'Don't worry about anything!'

In the morning I woke up when Joan came into my room. She didn't have to tell me. Anna had died.

5

AMONG THE REINDEER

The first rule of dating a reindeer herder: never ask how long they'll be away. This is because they never know; comings and goings are based on the weather and the condition of the herd, two factors that can never be accounted for by the ticks of a clock.

Áilu is gone frequently, sometimes for weeks on end, throughout the year. He is making sure that his reindeer are safe from predators and that they have enough food. While he's away, because of an utter lack of cell reception high in the mountains, there is no way to get in touch or check in. I carry on with my schoolwork, spending outside hours visiting his sisters or Yoko and others from our class, wondering when he might return.

Only about 10 per cent of reindeer-herding Sámi still herd full-time – and in Norway, one must be Sámi to own reindeer at all. Reindeer herding is considered a traditional Sámi livelihood that has gone on in the high Arctic in one form or another for thousands of years and is as much cultural as it is commercial.

Even though reindeer herders now live in modern society – using cell phones, Internet, GPS and high-powered snowmobiles as would anyone else – the modern world still remains an assault on the livelihoods of reindeer herders, who need land and freedom of movement of the reindeer to keep their work viable. Numbers of herders are steadily declining for many reasons: an increase in mining activity and wind farms that take up grazing land and disrupt natural ecosystems, not to mention the increasing impact of climate change. Although the Sámi – as is the case with most indigenous cultures – are deft at dealing with the unpredictability of nature, in recent years climate change has been increasingly devastating to herders and their economy; the primary reason being that reindeer feed on lichen, and when the snow comes, and melts, and freezes hard, and then more snow arrives, the reindeer can't get to their food source. Herders are forced to buy food to keep the herds alive through harsh winters. The feed is expensive, and a bad winter to a reindeer herder can be as disastrous as a bad season for a farmer with floods or crop rot.

There is always a threat of something new from the industrial world around the corner. A major rail line is proposed to cut through large swaths of the melting Arctic in years to come. In the economically depressed town of Kautokeino, there's talk of outside interest in crypto-currency-mining server farms, giant computing systems that run hot and are less costly to run in places that are frozen half the year, cutting cooling costs and lowering overheads. The first European data centre for Facebook is in Luleå, on the edge of the Swedish Arctic. And in addition to development, there is also the ongoing, and often unwelcome, involvement of the Norwegian government and the reindeer administration which, in the name of ecological management, dictates how many reindeer each owner can have in a herd. Many herders see this as bureaucratic interference in something they've been doing from time immemorial. But because reindeer are part of Sámi identity, no matter the challenges, reindeer herding is still an integral part of life in parts of the north, even for people with day jobs.

At no time is this more obvious than when the reindeer go in the fence, as it's called, to be inoculated, castrated, separated for marking or slaughter, and generally accounted for. It is a community event, with different *siida* (collectives) coming together for days at a time to work before the winter sets in. When Áilu's reindeer are ready to come in the fence, I go to join him, on a break from school, an hour outside our village.

The reindeer live free in the wild apart from now, when they are wrangled from the tundra into a huge circular wooden enclosure. The herders and other owners stand watching them for hours, occasionally pulling one out with their *suohpan*, the Sámi word for a lasso. Reindeer are marked by patterns of notches cut into their ears, called marks, unique to every owner: herders have an uncanny ability to see and identify a mark from a distance on a fast-moving creature. I stand in the fence, mesmerized by the hundreds of beasts circling the muddy enclosure, a blur of antlers, mud and hooves.

Inside this larger fence, the herders have to identify their reindeer before they are split into more manageable groups and herded into a smaller fence. Fifteen of us unfurl a giant green plastic tarpaulin and run in the direction of the gate, ushering the reindeer towards it. As many as fifty of these subsets can be broken off in one day.

Inside the smaller fence, entire families stand around the burlap-lined walls. Áilu's mother is here, a tiny woman, as are many other matriarchs who have grown up herding. The bulls are castrated and their antlers shorn down; if they weren't, they would mate to the point of exhaustion, leaving themselves ill-equipped to handle the brutal winters. Others are inoculated, which requires one person to hold the reindeer by its antlers while another sticks in the needle. Being big-boned, I take easily to the task of grabbing the antlers of the reindeer in the smaller enclosure, holding them so that Áilu can give them an inoculation or make a mark on their fur.

Some reindeer are selected for slaughter and sent into separate enclosures. Nearly every part of the animal is used, from skins and fur for warmth and clothing to bones for Sámi handicraft. Antlers and skins are often sent to Finland to be processed, and then sometimes on to Asia, where the antlers are thought to have a Viagra-like power. It is not acceptable to ask how many reindeer someone owns; it would be like asking how much they have in their savings account, and reindeer are a form of currency. This concept comes to life for me one day when Áilu's daughter, Ida, calls to say she is having car problems and will require an expensive repair. 'I must take a reindeer to get the car fixed,' Áilu tells me worriedly, meaning that some of his reindeer will have to be sold.

Outside of the fence, many of the reindeer are loaded on to a wooden-slatted livestock truck, bound for the slaughterhouse called Finnmark Rein on the rim of the south side of the village, and where Áilu also works butchering in the busy autumn. He is known for his speed.

From the outset, I hate the sight of the giant transport truck and the smell of urine and the clanging of hooves and the knowingness of the fear the animals are experiencing. Reindeer have very little fat and the meat quickly becomes adrenaline-filled, so you can literally taste the fear, a bitter, tough taste, which is why they are quickly taken to their end.

Those outside the fence that are not taken to the slaughterhouse are reindeer likely for personal use by individual families. They are killed with a cut to the neck followed by one to the heart. It takes a minute at most. I understand the Sámi respect for reindeer, having grown up among the farmers of the Midwest, but witnessing my first killing brings up a flood of emotion, and I have to hide behind a truck to cry. I don't want to appear weak or sentimental, but I also feel ashamed. I've always been a meat-eater, yet the reality of how a living thing becomes meat has never been brought home in such a primal way.

After work in the fence, the remainder of the reindeer are set free onto the tundra where the herders will move with them through the winter, making sure they are safe and able to get through the snow to feed on lichen. Although it is late, the slaughtered reindeer must be butchered, and we spend the night in the brumal cold, gutting them under lights run from a generator, their insides steaming in the icy air. I wait with Áilu in his family's *lávvu*, eating reindeer meat boiled in water and drinking the broth, earthy and gamey. Outside, the first hints of the aurora borealis appear as pale green wisps in the sky.

Work in the fence will continue for days, as batches of reindeer are brought in from the tundra. Each night, the auroras grow brighter and stronger, and I return to work with another *siida*, along with my Sámi language classmates, as we are now learning the language related to reindeer herding, including parts of the reindeer and what food is made with which parts, from blood pancakes to marrow bones.

The work is repetitive and exhausting and filled with hours of waiting: for reindeer to be brought in the fence, for them to be separated, for them to be transported away. But engaging in the work is important to me; when I arrived in Sápmi it was, in part, to become closer to a culture with which I shared some genetic connection, and therefore hoped to find belonging; now I can see that this was ridiculous, and more importantly, entirely irrelevant. I am beginning to understand that, in Kautokeino, there is great scepticism about anyone from the outside – people whose parents, and great-grandparents, and other family members are not known, their names, where they came from, the work they did, their stories. Here, known history and familial connections are everything. They give one meaning and context. Nothing else matters.

Learning to work with the reindeer and trying to learn the language is becoming an act of respect as much as it is desire for inclusion and acceptance. Respect for the culture in which I am living and also for Áilu in particular. We share so little in common – no cultural references and virtually no norms that would be standard in American life. This is not a relationship where showing up as a good partner means buying things or having lengthy discussions about feelings or sharing in career aspirations or future trajectories or a joint mortgage and a twenty-year plan. It is about sharing the burden of work without complaint. It means not showering for three days or chopping wood or standing out on the tundra for days waiting for the herd to be brought in and standing in the freezing fence for hours on end to inoculate the hundredth reindeer. This is devotion, and this is what matters here. This is what it means to be with a reindeer herder; you are not just with the person, but the life and culture that come with it.

I am slowly starting to learn that this is also why there are very few women from the outside with Sámi reindeer-herding men. I am new in the village, but I know of only one other non-Sámi woman with a herder – Marit, Áilu's sister-in-law, a hardy Norwegian from the south married to his oldest brother, a reindeer herder named Piera. Marit and Piera have five kids together, yet they are never in the fold of the rest of Áilu's family, even though Marit is warm and engaging, and capable of any amount of work in the fence or sewing *gákti*, the traditional Sámi dress, or teaching her kids about nature. Marit does not come to coffee in the *lávvu* on weekends with Áilu's sisters or work in the fence with the rest of the family; I also never see her at Áilu's mother's house, though they live next door to each other and share pasture for the reindeer. Marit and her kids keep a distance from the rest of Áilu's family, and I don't understand why.

I continue to spruce up our ancient apartment in the best way that I can, given limited options. Because my experience of Kautokeino is still largely relegated to what Áilu shares, I'm completely unaware that there are modern shops just two hours away in Alta. I buy a purple flowered oilcloth from a giant roll in the local general store for the kitchen, and in a box containing a jumble of second-hand cast-offs donated to Áilu, I find two 1970s abstract expressionist oil paintings, ten by ten inches, a muddle of browns and creams. They are utterly out of place but remind me of art I love, and I decide to hang them, using a black six-inch Prada pump – brought with me in case I ever had to travel for a meeting – that has found new utility here as a hammer. I dutifully make coffee every day, waiting for visitors, who usually end up being other reindeer herders who come and linger for hours with Áilu, murmuring in Sámi, talking about reindeer or watching football on TV. One day an older herder, a kind and avuncular man named Johan Ante, comes from the neighbouring village of Mieron, ten kilometres away, but Áilu isn't home. I fix Johan Ante coffee, and because my Sámi can't seem to get past the level of a three-year-old, our conversation ends after some talk of the weather and the fact that I'm American and that I've made coffee, and I find myself, for two hours, tensely watching the Princess Diana *E! True Hollywood Story* with him, with Norwegian subtitles, for no particular reason other than it's what came on and I felt it would be rude to change the channel.

In our off time, Áilu enjoys taking me round to his family for coffee, where we sit and engage in small talk and I practise my Sámi. But really, most of our relationship is about working. Áilu's hours are filled with work, if not with the reindeer then doing the work that is required to support reindeer herding itself – from painting houses and doing small repairs for the kommune, to butchering in the slaughterhouse or messengering a package or two to a nearby village. His only real relaxation comes from playing in a football league on the giant pitch near our house. I work trying to keep the house clean and learning the language, helping Áilu in between doing some remote consulting via Skype and email, work that perplexes Áilu and he articulates as 'yelling into the computer'.

Áilu dreams of going to New York and asks me many questions about my former home. We talk about visiting one day, which is very much a fantasy, given that to leave the reindeer for any length of time would be an impossibility for him. If we were to marry, Áilu would have to go to America. In the most traditional Sámi marital custom, a groom and his family must visit the family of the bride on the occasion of an engagement; it is a nod to the idea of two clans joining. I go into mental hysterics, followed by utter sadness, at the idea of Áilu's family gathering together their money and travelling across the North Atlantic in earnest and arriving at my father's and Joan's upscale retirement community in Maine in their traditional *gáktis*, only to be met by Joan slamming the door on their faces because she is 'over-stimulated'. It has happened to others before.

We never talk much about my family in detail. First, Sámi people do not discuss private matters outside of the family: this is completely verboten. Áilu knows discussion of my own family makes me sad, and for him to understand without subsequent details that I lost my mother at an early age was enough for him. In Sámi culture mothers are everything; the culture simply could not go on without them. They are the centre of the universe and paragons of strength and survival, raising the children, working with the reindeer, making all of the food and intricate traditional dress, teaching the kids about nature and survival in it, passing down the customs and stories. Mothers and children are very rarely apart, and

I've noticed that Áilu's sisters never leave the kids for a 'night out' or to take a break.

We walk on the tundra, which is one of my favourite things to do together, feeling my feet on the spongy, loamy ground, making me feel as if I could trek for a hundred miles without noticing. We share jokes and discuss the nature around us. The sky feels so thin and sharp here – utterly different from anything I have ever experienced – with no perceived distance between the earth and space. It's mostly so quiet you can hear the whoosh of a bird's wings or the crackle of giant hares leaping through the bushes – hares the size of goats and ptarmigans that explode out of bushes in glorious clusters. Áilu is funny and quite superstitious; he's full of beliefs and sayings that are sometimes his and sometimes more widely held Sámi idioms. It is getting colder in autumn and I'm sneezing a lot, so naturally my favourite saying, which he uses all the time, is 'if you sneeze three times, you'll be rich'.

One day we are out walking and come home to find that I have lost the key to the apartment; this is problematic because they are skeleton keys and there are only two. Áilu is terribly worried about it and we rip the apartment apart, searching through bulky coat pockets and behind furniture and in drawers. It is nowhere to be found and Áilu finally tells me that he must call someone – a woman who is a finder of lost objects. 'But you must not tell people,' he says to me sternly. Shamans – spiritual people who are healers and often deeply prescient – have always existed in Sámi culture, which was historically based in animism, until Christian missionaries snuffed out its open practice in sometimes brutal and oppressive ways. There are shamans throughout Sápmi – women and men who have been known to heal bleeding with a touch or foretell the future – but they don't advertise or have psychic hotlines or make any public display of their ability. The historical fear of discussing such a topic might have made Áilu ambivalent about sharing it, but for me it was perfectly natural. When my mother died, even as a small child, I knew she was gone and dead, but I believed her to be in another place, one I could not see or touch, in much the same way one can't see the Internet but it exists. Subsequently, my whole life I've been curious about mysteries that cannot be seen. Through the years I've observed many frauds and crackpots but also met several people who not only comforted me and gave me clarity, but also had an unmistakable gift of prescience. I find it perplexing and sad that science is often so narrow and dismissive of the possibility of these sorts of concepts. It feels a loss to believe that one holds all the answers in a world in which we continue to know so little.

Áilu calls the woman and paces around the apartment, nodding his head and saying 'juo, juo, juo', or 'yes, yes, yes', as if following instructions. He walks into the entry-way to our apartment and pulls out my many-pocketed North Face jacket, which had already been examined and found to have no key. He listens intently then feels the lining of the jacket, and finds the key in a small inside pocket, says thank you and hangs up the phone. I ask him what she said. 'The key is in the blue jacket of a foreigner, near the door, in a small pocket.'

I was not astonished, just very pleased to have found the key.

Áilu's parents' house is a short walk away from ours, and one Saturday I join his mother to learn how to do *gámasneaskin*, or the preparing of reindeer skins to be made into shoes for winter, cosy fur boots lined with wool and dried reeds, and literally the warmest and best shoes I have ever worn. First the skins must be softened, and this requires gently scraping them on a slanted board with a small-serrated tool that takes off the hard and tough portion of the skin. The work is exacting and more difficult than it seems, and can take hours of tiny movements to soften a small patch of hide. I sit with Áilu's mother out back in the crisp autumn air, the yard littered with snowmobiles and sleds and petrol cans and wood and fences, Čáhppe the dog by my side. The first time I'd visited Kautokeino I was privately appalled by what I saw as junk in everyone's yards, wondering how people lived with so much chaos. But I would come to see that every single thing in a yard had a reason for being there. It also probably did not help that Inger Marit was the mother of three reindeer herders, all of whom kept most of their gear in the yard. Áilu's mother is kind and encouraging, and although we still are limited in our means of communication, I am able to understand by watching her work.

Mostly, I visit with Áilu's sisters if I want company, lingering over coffee as they go about their days, a gaggle of children always around. Their level of English is a great blessing to me, in that they are able to explain many customs and traditions and the reasons why things are done in a certain manner, and they want to share their culture with me and help me with learning the language. There are profound differences in even the smallest interactions, so ingrained that we don't realize they are unique ways of doing things – me as an American or them as Sámi. On one of my first visits to Áilu's sister

Risten's house, when it was time to take our leave, I went into all of the rooms saying goodbye to the children one by one and hugging them, which is something I would do in America before leaving any party or gathering – and most especially as a Midwesterner, where there are multiple stages of a very protracted goodbye, starting with the first announcement that it's probably time to go, followed by a second goodbye, a hug, a goodbye at the door, more chitchat, the real goodbye and then the wave once out the door. The kids looked perplexed and one even horrified as I gave them an abbreviated version of my typical American departure. Áilu told me why later, laughing. 'They thought you were dying or leaving forever.' Sámi comings and goings just happen, quietly, without fanfare or announcement.

I want desperately to make meals and have people over; dinner parties were one of my favourite things, a way to get to know people and break bread and have long conversations. Except, I am learning that people in the north don't have others over for dinner as a general rule, and I find this a difficult adjustment. Families also do not have set mealtimes; mostly food is laid out on the hob and everyone eats when they're hungry, on his or her own schedule. Plus, I loved cooking, but Áilu did not seem interested in food other than boiled or dried reindeer and butter. At Thanksgiving, I am excited to find a turkey at the local grocery store, and attempt to make an American feast – with mashed potatoes, green beans and *tyttlebar*, the tart red berry that is an ideal stand-in for cranberry sauce. Áilu tries his hardest to show an interest but is set in his ways and mostly uninterested in the food, and anything new for that matter. I am left with piles of leftovers.

With winter nearing, the mornings and the evenings are becoming darker, with night encroaching little by little until it will be full Polar night, without the sun rising at all. At night the stars are so clear and bright that you can often catch a glimpse of one falling, or bright white pinpricks that slowly travel across the horizon, which I disappointedly learn are not unknown planets or major stars but satellites junking up the pristine night sky – more than two thousand of them. The mornings are the most difficult, waking up in cold blackness and a freezing apartment in which a fire has not yet been stoked in the living room, with ice lining even the insides of the window frames, gathering in crevices and chilling the laminate floors. I sleep in a fleece pullover and sweatpants, and when it becomes really cold, with only jeans to wear to school – which anyone used to winter climes can tell you are the worst clothing to have in snow and wet – I walk to the village centre, and still not understanding that there are places to buy snow pants, I find a pair of heavy children's tights in purple cable knit, take them home and sew them in to leg warmers, looking something like a demented Jennifer Beals from the movie *Flashdance* as I walk up the hill to Sámi school every morning wearing cut-up tights meant for a six-year-old. In public.

Our first set of exams is near; we will have to do a question-and-answer portion with an invigilator and I could not be more nervous. I practise with Yoko in her tiny apartment in student housing for hours on end, and on the same day that we take our orals, we are both thrilled to find out that we have made it past our first Sámi language class.

The local TV station, NRK Sápmi, comes to interview us, and I tell the interviewer that it is very cold in Sápmi and that if you live here it's very important to learn Sámi. I might as well have been on the BBC Áilu is so proud; my interview is run on *Ođđasat*, the Sámi language evening news, twice. I feel the triumph of validation. I am starting to feel as if I belong.

6

AWAY

Indianapolis has a bohemian area known as Broad Ripple, a suburban village near a canal that's part of the White River. The area took its name from a poem of the same name by the great Indiana poet James Whitcomb Riley. The canal is nothing like one you'd imagine in the original Venice, in that Broad Ripple's main features, beyond the canal, are a surfeit of mallard ducks and lush ash trees and an old graffitied train trestle where you'd go to sneak cigarettes with your friends after dark. In Broad Ripple, fading yet beloved staples of childhood coexisted with a vibrant and growing eighties counter-culture; Ed Schock's hobby shop and the Roslyn bakery where you'd get your coffee cake for after church on Sundays are juxtaposed with a 1930s picture house turned nightclub called the Vogue and a punk rock clothing store called Future Shock, chock-a-block with Doc Martens and Anarchy T-shirts and started by a Liverpudlian thrash metal bass player named Tufty, who inexplicably made his way to the Midwest and settled. Broad Ripple was an eighties-era magnet for kids who did not fit in to the traditional Indiana adolescent experience and trajectory; kids who weren't on varsity teams or in debate club or headed for a certain future of good grades and mortgages and the right golf club. If the John Hughes film *The Breakfast Club* had taken place in Indiana, and not in the neighbouring state of Illinois, Ally Sheedy's brooding, kohl-eyed character surely would have proudly been from Broad Ripple.

At the beating heart of Broad Ripple, right on the main drag, was Café Espresso, and this was where most of the outsiders hung out after school, nursing gallons of cheap coffee and playing checkers and studying and smoking cigarettes. The place had dark panelled wood walls and a giant fireplace with seating around it, giving it a cosy ski-chalet feel, and there were punks, and skaters, and musicians, as well as a handful of guys from the local chapter of Alcoholics Anonymous, who would bravely beeline past the Alley Cat bar behind the café, coming in after meetings, and stay for hours holding court, nursing mugs of warm black coffee and copious numbers of Marlboro Reds smoked to the nub. The café always buzzed with comings and goings, local drama and a sense of a community of outcasts and fabulous people – or at least people who one day would be fabulous – and I found the café's draw irresistible. I'd spend most of my free time after school or in off-shifts from Supercuts at the café, studying or listening to the stories of some of the hard-boiled lives that made me feel ordinary and, therefore, normal. I loved hearing one man in his sixties in particular, named Bill, a published and serious writer, talk about his drinking days and reckless adventures hanging out with strippers with names like Lottie the Body and Yvette Evil – the former a woman who could apparently shoot ping-pong balls out of her vag – or his dream to visit Charles Bukowski in San Pedro, because Bukowski was the patron saint of writerly alcoholics who had experienced hard-lived lives, survived and transformed their hurt and misadventure into poetry. Richard, another café patron, was a mild-mannered computer programmer and Anglophile who shared stories about his annual trips to visit family in England and seemed to calm any drama that might happen in the café – and he always had time for you if you had a problem or needed to talk something through, lending a measured rationality to any crisis. Rich C was another AA guy in his early fifties, dark-skinned and lanky, who rode a gorgeous Harley and was a magnet to any woman over thirty, full of swagger and oozing sexuality in his black biker jacket and steel-toed boots.

The women at work kept a close eye on me as I began to step into this new world. It felt like Kristy and Carol and the Supercuts ladies were becoming stern yet loving surrogate mothers, involving themselves in my comings and goings, asking after my school performance, monitoring the people I dated, and generally making sure I kept in line – a nurturing concern that increased after Anna died, as if they instinctively knew I needed guidance. Carol, who came from a large and warm Catholic family, loved her mother back in South Bend Indiana more than just about any person on earth, and drove the two and a half hours north to see her almost every other weekend. Carol took a protective role with me. 'My God, Laura, I will not allow you to go out with that scum!' she said once about a boy I liked. Marc, the owner of all the Supercuts franchises, who lived in Los Angeles, came to visit the Indiana shops and offered me a place to stay with his girlfriend if I ever wanted to see California. There was a running joke about me being the youngest person ever to work at the Supercuts because I was only fifteen and needed a work permit when I started, which Carol had to scramble to secure. In its own way, life was wonderful: I had access to all the Paul Mitchell Freeze and Shine hairspray I could want and people cared about me.

One Saturday, I arrived for my usual shift and was surprised to see a gorgeous redhead standing at one of the haircutter's stations, going decidedly off uniform from our bright-orange and electric-blue smocks with the Supercuts logo. She was wearing cream pants and a cream turtleneck, her hair cut into a pristine angular bob. She wore bright red lipstick and had a tidy French manicure and looked like she belonged in *Vogue* magazine rather than giving a scruffy groundskeeper a number-two clipper cut for seven dollars. I had no idea what to make of her, a vision that seemed strangely and effortlessly conversant and interested in the finer points of grass reseeding.

Her name was Mary and she was an international flight attendant who was taking a second job to make extra money, because apparently flight attendants weren't well paid. Mary had been all over the world and had an air of sophistication that was inviting rather than exclusionary. 'I needed a little extra cash to keep up my lifestyle, and the sugar daddy wasn't cutting it!' she said with a wink, and I was unsure if it was to be taken as a joke or in seriousness. Everyone regarded Mary with trepidation in the beginning, but it was obvious that she wasn't afraid of hard work and grit and greasy hair and shitty customers that sometimes wanted the world along with their desire for a haircut that would transform them into Farrah Fawcett. We learned slowly, through guarded anecdotes, that Mary had not come from money: she had ascended to the finer things. On breaks in the back room, Mary would tell me about her 'turns', as she'd call them, to Paris and Milan and explain high fashion and good skincare to me. It never sounded like bragging. She gave me a primer, starting with Hermès and the cost and provenance of the exquisite brown silk scarf with bicycles on it that she'd throw over her cream-coloured coat when she was leaving, the fresh waft of Diva perfume that she'd spritzed on scenting the room. 'Thank God for duty free!' she'd say, laughing. Mary was full of things to teach me and I was an eager student.

One rainy Wednesday night at the Supercuts, there were no customers, and out of the blue, Mary decided that I should see New York City as an essential part of life training – that and she thought I'd be a good travel companion. She seemed to have forgotten that I was only sixteen, and I did not remind her. 'Let's do that next weekend,' she murmured, in a tone so casual she could just as easily have been suggesting we grab some Big Macs from the McDonald's up the street when our shifts ended. We could stay with another flight attendant in her studio apartment on the Upper East Side.

Mary was able to travel almost anywhere she wanted at a moment's notice if seats were available on the airline for which she worked; she arranged a dirt-cheap ticket for me. The only issue was my parents – but they were largely disengaged from my comings and goings, and so I found myself, at sixteen years old, in the middle of New York

City with Mary, dancing to Jennifer Holliday blasting out 'One Night Only' over the speakers at a gay club in the West Village, seeing men make out with other men for the first time with shock and awe, mesmerized by spectacular drag queens glammed to the hilt, and possibly the most gorgeous flight attendants I'd ever seen. Any fear of getting caught flying halfway across the country or being underage in a club seven hundred miles from home was utterly eclipsed by being hardly able to believe what was happening. I was home by Sunday, the idea of bigger cities and bigger adventures firmly rooted in my mind.

I always knew I wanted to leave Indiana, an itch that was growing stronger by the day since Anna had died, a desire that only increased once I'd travelled to New York. I no longer felt I connected much with anyone at high school because it was hard to be light and carefree, attending home football games or trying to get into popular girls clubs, a rite of passage in my high school that was brutally hierarchical and exclusionary. Grief and darkness still sat inside me, existing side by side with an enormous desire to explore and see the world, and everything else felt restrictive and superfluous. I coexisted, more than anything else, with Dad and Joan; they were unengaged with my performance at school or future plans, and more than ever, home felt like a place I no longer belonged. I felt much older than my sixteen years. Outside of Supercuts and the café, I was rudderless, except for the newspaper staff at school, the one place where I did connect, and where smart kids and outcasts had some sense of kinship and purpose.

I was writing for the school paper and also contributing to the world of hard-hitting feature journalism with groundbreaking articles with titles like 'To Perm or Not to Perm – Is It Your Question?' in the monthly Supercuts magazine, circulated in haircutting reception areas from Boise to Duluth, and many Midwestern towns in between. It was the first place that ever paid me to write something, and it gave me a sense of pleasure and accomplishment. Carol and Kristy and the other haircutters proudly pointed out to customers when I had an article in the magazine. 'We need to be careful she doesn't get a big head,' Kristy joked.

I loved the attention. I wanted to do it more.

At one point, my brother-in-law Chuck, now stationed in Warsaw as the bureau chief there for the *Los Angeles Times*, suggested that I should pursue my interest in journalism and look into the University of Missouri, his alma mater, known for its journalism programme, or Northwestern, where my paternal grandfather had gone to journalism school and had a career of renown as an editor for the Associated Press and the Latin American affairs editor for *US News and World Report*. Linda was an accomplished journalist in her own right, and she had gone to New York University. I looked up to them both – I loved that they took an interest in my writing, sending me spectacular essays from the literary journal *Granta*, like Bill Bryson's gem 'Fat Girls in Des Moines', and critiquing my work. I knew it was what I wanted to do.

Conversations about college made me queasy because they highlighted the fact that I would be asking for something, and this in turn made me vulnerable to an overt reminder that I wasn't worth any investment – or anything at all, for that matter – and an attempt to make a request would almost inevitably be met with not just a no, but a backlash of rejection. But college – this was one instance in which I couldn't just keep my head down or do it alone. College cost money and I knew this was something my parents weren't likely to support, given the way I'd seen all of my siblings struggle – from Will selling his plasma to pay rent when he was at school to Mark going away entirely into the military. I decided to talk it over with my dad, first, and share my ambitions with him. I knew that, in his own way, he cared about me and education had obviously been important in his becoming a doctor. It was a risk to ask, but a scholarship would be impossible, given that my father was wealthy, and I was unlikely to be able to raise the funds for these fancy out-of-state places from my $3.35-an-hour job at Supercuts, no matter how many shifts I worked. I felt selfish wanting something so big for myself, but I had to try. So I steeled myself, and as we sat at the kitchen table one evening, I told my dad how much I wanted to go to Northwestern, and that I needed to know if it was a reasonable goal and something for which I should aim. He listened carefully and calmly and told me he'd consider it, but the time for pondering was short-lived. Joan came to me the next morning. 'Who do you think you are? We will never pay for college at one of those places. You live in a fantasy world. Stop manipulating your father. You'll go to a state school and you'll study marketing.'

The conversation was closed. But something had changed: other people were starting to give me a sense of value, and all the years of being told I was not worthy and believing it were giving way to the tiniest bud of empowerment – or maybe it was just wilfulness. I was developing a greater sense of self through my friendships at work and at the café, but this was a double-edged sword. I'd asserted myself in asking about college, and the dreaded scenario had played out much as I'd expected it to. Joan became more dour and threatening, my day-to-day existence met with shut doors and the silent treatment and a seething disdain that was as solid and tangible as a cinder block. An air of foreboding hung in the house whenever I was around, making me not want to be there and filling me with crippling anxiety. It made me more sure that I needed to go before I was sent. I'd seen it with my sister and both of my brothers; I was a Galloway and it was only a matter of time before I was sent packing, so I decided to be proactive.

I was just finishing my junior year. In a stroke of luck, a waitress at the café had just rented a basement apartment in Broad Ripple and needed a roommate. I could join her along with her ferret. The apartment was dirt cheap and across from Broad Ripple High, made famous because David Letterman and the American newscaster Jane Pauley had gone there. Richard the computer guy, now a good friend and sort of big-brother figure, lived one street over in case there was any trouble. The place had two bedrooms and a mouldy shared bathroom. The ferret would have the run of the place. All things considered, it sounded ideal.

I woke up one morning and told Joan as plainly as possible. 'I think I'm mature enough to move out and I'd like to go.'

'That's fine,' she said, with no emotion. 'When are you leaving?'

'Tonight?'

My father made no protest, and in fact decided to help with the rent. This hurt me; but the hurt was momentary when it dawned on me that this was my dad's way of getting me out of the house to some sort of emotional safety, as he'd suggested years before. And so I went, along with some old Le Menu plastic microwaveable frozen dinner plates, a fork, a blue futon bed from Pier 1 Imports, and a chair and a giant lamp that were donated by Dad and Joan.

*

Spring bled into summer. I was living with Dawn the waitress and her pet ferret in our abysmal basement apartment which flooded when it rained, seeping into my futon. The ferret sneaked into my room and bit my toes at night with its pin-sharp teeth – it was possibly the first time I didn't love an animal. Dawn was in her early twenties and had extremely loud sex, the sound of which was unabated even through her shut bedroom door, and which I tried hard to ignore by putting pillows over my head and listening to the Cure as loudly as possible on my Walkman. I drove to the Supercuts for work every day and finished high school a semester early with a performance so lacklustre that I'm not even sure to this day that I actually graduated – my will to apply myself to my studies evaporated when I didn't feel like there was any reason to aim high. My grades were enough to get me into a satellite campus for Indiana University in Indianapolis, an affordable state school, where I started college early, thinking I might transfer to the bigger Bloomington campus later.

Occasionally, I saved up my money to call Linda and Chuck in Warsaw for a crackly three- or four-minute call. During one of the calls, both suggested that I apply to Chuck's paper, the *Los Angeles Times*, to see if I might get a coveted summer job there as a copy messenger. At that time it was one of the largest and most respected papers in the world. I was too young and inexperienced to land an internship, as powerful and full of promise as my Supercuts magazine stories on finding the right shampoo for your hair type might have been. But each year a handful of messengers were selected, and Chuck's daughter Rachel had just started her job as one. 'It would be great for you to be at the paper for the summer, to experience a major newsroom and see if being a journalist is something you really want,' Chuck said. Linda, who was on the outs with Joan, also thought I needed to get out of Indianapolis.

Waiting for a response on my application to the *Times* brought a sense of anticipation that was torturous and delicious in equal measure; I wonder how we ever survived waiting for the arrival of important news before the instant gratification of email. Each day I ran home between school and work to check the metal postbox in the lobby of our dingy apartment building; each day I was greeted with expectant looks at work or the café, wondering if any news had come. It was as if this news meant as much to everyone as it did to me. And then one day a letter arrived from the *Los Angeles Times*, on embossed manila paper, typed and with an ink signature that smudged when I put my wet finger on it, just to make sure it was real. It was signed by the managing editor, George Cotliar, offering me the job.

I felt as if I might explode with joy, because this paper represented promise and invited possibility and chances. My future had arrived.

7

BARGU (WORK)

Since I've arrived in Kautokeino, I've made money from some long-distance consulting work, continuing a job organizing a conference for a magazine to keep me going financially. I started the project in New York, but most of the work is solitary; it largely involves research, reading and reaching out to potential speakers via email and Skype, and miraculously, no one ever thinks to ask me where I am located – it is just assumed that I am working from New York, Skyping in for meetings when necessary. It is strange and even funny to be on a high-level strategic call about the future of healthcare in America while Áilu stands carving dried reindeer in the kitchen. The money isn't much, but it's enough to give Áilu my share of the rent and the utilities each month. My expenses are now small, and a world away from my overwhelming New York existence, at the centre of which were massive rent and health insurance. Now most of our food comes from the reindeer and I'm not even using a cell phone; if someone needs to reach me they usually Skype or send me an email. People often have a mental picture about what living in the Arctic means in terms of remoteness and isolation, perhaps thinking that everyone lives in an igloo, and are almost invariably taken aback to learn that the Internet is better and faster in Sápmi than anywhere I'd experienced in the States.

But now, my project is ending and, with no cushion to speak of, I need to make money. During a visit to Karasjok, Stein suggests that I talk to the rector of the university where I studied Sámi about helping the university to raise its media profile and perhaps attract more visibility on the international stage.

My profession in New York was as a media strategist, helping thought leaders and institutions get the word out about their work and ideas. I worked on one project in particular, from the start, as the head of media relations for a conference that put its talks online, and it became a wildly successful global brand, familiar to almost everyone. I love my work and spend hours talking to Stein about the challenges I see with indigenous rights and media visibility. 'This could be a good connection!' Stein says enthusiastically, and tells me that he's already told the rector that I could be an asset to the university in its efforts.

The Sámi allaskuvla opened in 1989, a university college built to promote Sámi language, culture and understanding, funded by the Norwegian state as part of a commitment to undoing the policies of Norwegianization, the national policy which pulled Sámis from their culture and language for several decades. The university began with key programmes to encourage the culture and language, including teacher education in Sámi language and Sámi research and studies ranging from *duodji*, Sámi handicraft, to courses on animal husbandry and Sámi journalism – the latter being vitally important, as an essential part of language survival and revitalization is the availability of mass media in the language in question. Norwegian National Broadcasting (NRK) has a branch named NRK Sápmi across from the university, as well as headquarters in Karasjok, from which an evening news programme, *Oddasat*, is broadcast, as well as children's programming and special reports fed into NRK nationally if the story is big enough. A radio station and a Sámi language newspaper named *Ávvir* are also headquartered in Kautokeino, and all of these efforts require trained reporters, thus the allaskuvla was growing in importance for aspiring journalists.

The university, a large wooden building in the Scandinavian modernist style, sits in the middle of the village on a hill, incongruous with its surroundings but somehow fitting as if it had always been there. The entire building has been constructed with Sámi culture and motifs in mind, and the result is dramatic and beautiful: frosted glass panelling for conference rooms etched with images of cloudberries and native plants; dramatic ramps leading up and down the floors of the building intended as a nod to the *lávvu*; and in the main area of the building, a wall of windows facing east, overlooking the village and its breathtaking expanse of tundra. In the massive cafeteria sits a gigantic wooden Sámi longboat, used as a serving table for large buffets, and an elegant manmade fireplace and seating area, also intended to evoke the inside of a cosy *lávvu*, an area for storytelling and visiting over a cup of coffee. Behind the library, on an upper floor and down a hidden corridor, are the Sámi Archives, a climate-controlled archive of Sámi history and important documents from books to pictures dating back as long as Sámi history has been recorded.

The university is giant, made to feel even bigger because there usually appears to be almost no one there. This isn't the case, of course, but because there are less than three hundred students, and less than a quarter of that at school at the same time, one is constantly left with the impression that it's empty, save for lunchtime, when staff holed up in their offices come out and sit at the long tables, chatting and having a meal and a cup of coffee. The university is one of the largest employers in the village, with a staff that vastly exceeded the number of students at any given time.

As far as I can decipher, the challenge for the university is that prospective students exist all across the Arctic of Sweden, Norway, Finland and the Kola Peninsula of Russia – most in places that are too far for commuting on a daily basis – and the marketing for the university has been limited. Marketing in general is not a strength in Sámi culture. I know that I would be no help in attracting more Sámi students to the university because I do not understand the barriers to attendance, and the subtle cultural reasons, but I do see a giant opportunity for the university to become a world-class cultural centre for the Sámi people, and perhaps other indigenous cultures. The school has a large and modern auditorium, and I can imagine a series of programmes in which authors and musicians and leaders can come and give lectures and performances, putting Kautokeino on the map.

An expat always has key moments where they become painfully aware of differences in culture, a learning curve which no books or Internet sites can adequately prepare them for. Of course, I bump into these moments all the time as I learn about life in Sápmi because absolutely everything is different: leaving your door open all the time and being ready for visitors; not having punctuated goodbyes; the fluidity of time and appointments ('I'll meet you at four' is a suggestion, not a directive). But nothing could really prepare me for meeting the rector of the Sámi allaskuvla, an imposing Russian Sámi woman named Jelena Porsanger.

She agrees to chat with me in the cafeteria – I use chat in the most general context possible because the meeting could best be described as me gushing animatedly to a concrete wall. We could not be more opposite: she a Russian Sámi who'd come from the Arctic, where immediate enthusiasm and familiarity – American traits baked in to me from birth, manifesting in this case in the form of verbal diarrhoea – inspire scepticism and even mistrust. I give Jelena an overview of my background and experience, mentioning the gathering that I'd worked with for several years that had become a global brand and was usually my calling card (but apparently had not yet made its way to the Arctic). Jelena sits, stony-eyed and unresponsive, speaking briefly of some work they are doing with e-learning, and then the conversation is unceremoniously over. I will clearly not be doing any project work for the university.

In New York, my identity was completely wrapped around having a high-powered job and important clients. It was the first thing anyone ever raised about me in conversation; in fact, in New York, and probably in the rest of America, it is the first thing that anyone asks about you after your name in a social situation – what line of work are you in? Now I am in a place where my CV and accomplishments mean nothing and get me nowhere. It is like being without a layer of skin and the effect is unsettling. I've always thought that, no matter how much I had in my bank account (or didn't), I'd always have my past work to help define my possibilities for the future. Not here. And I also didn't understand something fundamental about Norwegian culture. In New York, if you aren't proactive and ambitious and assertive, you aren't fit for purpose. In Norway, if you trumpet your accomplishments, you are a braggart and you are castigated. There is even a term for it, known well throughout Scandinavia: Janteloven, or The Law of Jante, which isn't an actual law, but a reference to an informal social code throughout the Nordics that dictates, among other things, that one shouldn't stand out.

My friend Per mentions it in passing on one telephone conversation, and I am fascinated to learn more because it will colour every interaction I have in Norway, as if a giant code has been revealed, even in this Sámi village – which is, after all, in Norway. The Law of Jante came from a satirical novel by a Danish Norwegian called Aksel Sandemose, penned in the 1930s and focused on a fictional town. The ten rules include:

1. You're not to think *you* are anything special.
2. You're not to think *you* are as good as *we* are.
3. You're not to think *you* are smarter than *we* are.
4. You're not to imagine yourself better than *we* are.
5. You're not to think *you* know more than *we* do.
6. You're not to think *you* are more important than *we* are.
7. You're not to think *you* are good at anything.

8. You're not to laugh at *us*.
9. You're not to think anyone cares about *you*.
10. You're not to think *you* can teach *us* anything.

I can immediately see that I've blown it with numbers 5, 7 and 10, and now I understand why the author of *The Xenophobe's Guide to the Norwegians*, which I'd thumbed through in the Oslo airport long ago, had jokingly written that if you complain about anything, Norwegians will think you are a foreigner, crazy or both. The Law of Jante!

*

Fall continues to creep into winter with speed; every day a little colder, a little darker, and it's harder to get out of bed in the morning. Áilu is gone more and more, getting ready for winter with the reindeer, fixing more fences (an ongoing job) and repairing snowmobiles. On most weekends, I walk over to his mother and father's house nearby, and go next door to visit Marit and Piera, sometimes with Áilu and sometimes alone. One Saturday, there is a light dusting of snow on the ground and, tired of studying, I decide to go for coffee with Marit. The house is a housekeeping disaster, which tends to happen when you have five kids and two dogs and are married to a reindeer herder. I like visiting her, though, because she is always bright and happy and loves to explain all things Norwegian. She fascinates me for more than a few reasons: she's a southern Norwegian from Trondheim who has had five kids with Piera, yet she has adapted to every part of Sámi culture, taking the kids into the fence and working with the reindeer, teaching them about animal husbandry, dressing them properly in elaborate Sámi clothing – which is no small feat for five kids – and basically surviving in a place not made for outsiders, even if they are Norwegian. Nothing seems to daunt her. She is the science teacher at the Sámi high school and she is also a delicious gossip who seems to know everything going on in the village, and so I learn more and more every time we are together. We speak in English and I think she's happy for the company; Áilu's sisters, save for one time we all had coffee when I first arrived, don't visit with Marit or interact, due to some family dispute that I'm too timid to ask about – all Áilu will say is that 'she thinks she knows everything'. Piera, Áilu's brother, is the oldest son in the family; he is a compact man, sinewy and tough, but with a ragingly good sense of humour and dancing blue eyes. Once on the tundra, waiting for the reindeer to come in, I was in the *lávvu* with Piera, who was sneaking rolled cigarettes because Marit did not approve. We sat in stitches of laughter as he told me about parts of the reindeer and how they are used commercially, and I suggested that hooves, one of the only non-perishable products that I could tell wasn't used, could be marketed as a male potency enhancement. He's fond of retelling me a story about an American English teacher that once came to the Sámi high school – from Los Angeles, of all places – in the 1980s, and who allegedly brought his pistol to class and would talk frequently and lovingly about his Cadillac back in America.

Marit and Piera have two dogs: a black female Lapsk Vallhund, – a Sámi reindeer-herding dog – named Čierggis, and a gigantic white and blond male Vallhund mix named Vilge, who is the father to Čierggis. Vilge is also a Sámi herding dog, and he is getting on in years but has a bellowing bark and is known as one of the best reindeer-herding dogs in the area. Čierggis generally goes out with Piera with the reindeer, which is unusual in that females aren't typically used for herding, – because 'then we'd be herding dogs, not reindeer!' Piera explains to me with his typical humour.

I am surprised to open Marit's front door to a gaggle of tiny puppies running amok; Čierggis had given birth a few weeks before, and here they are now, jumping on their grandfather Vilge, who gives a grumpy and half-hearted grunt as they pull on his ears, running to Čierggis for milk, and generally leaping over each other, tumbling, wrestling, chewing and frolicking in the most endearing scene ever. You couldn't help but want to scoop them up one by one and cuddle them, nuzzling their soft fur and tiny little foot pads, soft as clay. These dogs will be adopted quickly; people know their line and that Piera is the owner. It makes me melancholy, understanding that these puppies will be relegated to lives of work, discipline and even hardship in some cases, because animals are mostly not seen as pets here. I cringe every time I walk by houses in Kautokeino with forlorn-looking Norwegian Elkhounds, of which there are many, and who are usually chained up or stuck in small enclosures, save for September and October, when they are taken out to hunt for moose. Sometimes in the evening, I go to the petrol station and buy hot-dogs, throwing them in the enclosures when it is dark enough not be seen, trying to show some kindness to these creatures. It is no life for an animal but here animals live at the service of people, even dogs. My one hope is that Marit will have oversight on who would make a good owner and who would not. She originally came to Kautokeino to breed sled dogs, and she knows much about them, their temperament and who would make the best matches. She has a kind heart.

*

I'm getting terribly worried about my money situation when, one day, a miracle happens: my brothers and I are unexpectedly included in the will of our great-uncle Arthur, a small sum of money bequeathed to each of us. It is enough to get me through winter and is totally unexpected.

Arthur was my mother's uncle, and he was diagnosed with lung cancer just as I left for Norway, dying soon after. His loss was difficult for us all. Arthur had always been a rock for my brothers when they had nowhere else to go, so much so that my father, when Arthur became ill, wrote him a letter thanking him for everything he'd done through the years. Arthur was a world-class musician with a doctorate in music, and was no-nonsense and crisp in his comportment in a way that is particular to older gay men of a generation that had to mask themselves. He adored my mother and she him, from what I understood, and I'd call him every week from New York, just to chat and feel some connection to family. Shortly before I'd left for Norway, Arthur and his boyfriend had visited from San Francisco. They loved New York, and came to see some Broadway shows and make their traditional visit to the Algonquin for martinis. One day we shared a long lunch, and perhaps somehow sensing that this might be the last time we'd meet, Arthur teared up, the first show of emotion that I'd ever seen him reveal. It took me aback. 'I wonder what your life might have been like had your mother lived,' he said softly. 'Everything would have been so … different.'

I miss him so, and am filled with love and appreciation for the fact that he remembered us in this way.

8

WESTWARD

Where would I live? How would I get to Los Angeles? I could hardly contain my excitement over the summer job, and I knew in my heart that I wouldn't be coming back to Indiana. Every preparation was a concrete step towards leaving and I revelled in the planning: going to the local automobile club on my own to get something called TripTiks to plan my driving route – before the Internet, this is how trips were planned, using paper maps laid out state by state, measuring driving distances each day, plotting where I'd stop and how long the trip would take and if there would be a motel nearby. I called Linda and Chuck in Warsaw to let them know that I'd got the job, and I was soon in touch with Chuck's daughter, Rachel, along with two other girls who also had copy messenger jobs in the summer and needed roommates, and so it was decided quickly that we would all live together. Rachel found an apartment off the Pasadena freeway, in a place called Highland Park. It was close to the *Times*, which was downtown. I started reading Joan Didion, the great chronicler of California, like crazy and listening to seventies music like the Eagles and Joni Mitchell, because these things conjured the Los Angeles I'd always imagined in my mind's eye: hot sun, palm trees, Laurel Canyon, freedom.

By this time, I'd told everyone about my job, except for Dad and Joan. I didn't tell them because I dreaded the reaction. I didn't live with them and my father was contributing money to me each month, but I was essentially on my own – especially emotionally. I'd learned a long time ago that part of surviving in my family was to not make any waves, especially not doing something that might make anyone express joy or enthusiasm. If you floated your balloon, it would be unceremoniously shot down. I lived in a state of confusion and wanting: I was terrified of displeasing Joan and her rejection, but I was still too naïve and needy to understand that pleasing her to the point of earning any kind of emotional safety or mother–daughter intimacy was a Sisyphean act. She and Linda, who had fought like cats on and off for years, were also currently on the outs, because Joan thought she and Chuck had too much influence over me. Joan wasn't interested in parenting me, but she was deeply interested in exercising control at all times.

I mustered up the courage to tell them of my plans, and Joan responded with a glaring snarl and words that came out flat and even, with no emotion, like the low growl of a cat before it attacks. 'You'll go to Los Angeles when hell freezes over,' she informed me, and then went silent. My reaction wasn't anger, because people with great shame don't believe they are entitled to such a powerful emotion. Instead I was sick to my stomach, full of a hopelessness that felt insurmountable and profound. A braver person would have said fuck it, I'm going! But

I had a lifelong fear of not doing what my parents told me because I was repeatedly told that I was a shameful person and a manipulator.

'Dammit, you're going!' Kristy said in the break room of the Supercuts, as she furiously took drags off of her Kool cigarette, her face red with anger. Kristy had seen me through my last year and a half of high school as a sort of de facto mother, calling me in sick to school when I needed to study, letting me stay at her house when she and her husband went out of town and things were too loud at the apartment. 'You don't even live at home!' And it was Kristy, then Carol, then Mary, then everyone at the Supercuts who told me I needed to do this. Linda and Chuck also told me. And everyone at the café – talking about Los Angeles had become a daily topic of discussion, and the enthusiasm was mounting all around. We were a tight-knit group of people, this village of outcasts, and a chance for one of us was a chance for all of us. Everyone else had the courage I did not, and they gave me ballast.

I finally mustered the nerve to tell Joan that I was going anyway and again felt sick to my stomach with fear – of rejection, of being ostracized. A week passed and I was in my basement apartment when there was a knock at the door. It was Dad and Joan. They'd never been to my apartment before, and there they were, standing in front of me. 'We have something for you,' Joan says. 'Come outside.' I hesitated, wondering if I was going to have a potato sack thrown over my head and be carted off to the Culver military academy. Instead, out front was a white Pulsar NX, a new used car. 'You'll need this to get to California,' my dad said. I was stunned.

I will never understand the about-face that took place on that late spring afternoon. Had challenging Joan caused her to relent? Had my father put his foot down? Did Joan decide that she loved me after all and I was her daughter? Did she want good things for me? I so wanted to believe that. My heart exploded on that day – with relief, anticipation and a gratitude that painted the sky and filled every single cell in my body. I was going.

The new used car came because my old car, a brown Datsun 810, was falling apart and would never make it to California safely. My dad had driven it for years before turning it over to me as my first car. It had been lovingly restored by a man named Mr Kelly, who had been a diabetes patient of my father's and who looked after all of us when my mother had died, driving us to appointments and staying at home with us when my dad worked late, before Joan entered our lives. My dad had always given Mr Kelly various odd jobs; after Dad had remarried, Mr Kelly cleaned our house and I'd sit in the garage on a short stepladder with him while he'd have a cigarette and a diet root beer, admonishing me not to tell my dad that he was smoking. Mr Kelly had a prosthetic wooden leg, which always stuck out in front of him, stick straight, and left him with a peculiar limp when he walked. His twin brother had shot off his original leg in an argument. He used to unhook the prosthetic and show me if I asked, and even once terrified a neighbourhood bully on my behalf by taking it off and waving it at her after she'd made me cry. Mr Kelly had stopped working for Dad and Joan some years back, save for fixing up the car, buffing it and polishing it and putting rims on the tyres. There were so few happy memories of my life after my mother died, and

Mr Kelly was one of them. I knew I had to say goodbye to him and tell him the car had served me well and that I was getting out of Indiana. I found him in the phone book and we met at a McDonald's. There were few words between us because I hadn't yet developed the vocabulary to tell him what was inside of me, and that I was so grateful for the love he'd shown all of the Galloway kids, from looking after me to showing up at Anna's funeral in largely segregated rural Indiana, sitting in the second row, tears in his eyes. 'I'm going to miss you,' was all I could muster over our Cokes. 'You take care now, you hear me?' And we had our last goodbye.

I was excited about driving to California, but as the days inched forward I became ambivalent about the drive itself. What if the car broke down in the middle of nowhere? What if I couldn't find a motel? Or a phone if I needed help? I'd never been on a trip by myself, without family, without friends, without anyone, and the reality of the journey was setting in. I was voicing my worries out loud at the café to Richard two days before my departure, and Bill, the writer, overheard me. 'Well hell, Laura, I'll go with you. I've always wanted to go to San Pedro and leave a six-pack for Charles Bukowski. Do you think you could drop me off there?' I didn't see why not, and like that, I had a travelling companion.

I wouldn't miss long hours standing at the reception desk or cleaning out dirty hair-comb water, but it was difficult to say goodbye to the women at the Supercuts – all of them. They had become friends, mentors and protectors, mothers who are others. They'd sheltered me when I needed comfort, given me good advice, taught me about the harshness and realities of life, created safety for me to be myself while at the same time keeping me in line, and it was a bond that I knew would never be broken, no matter how much our lives might change – and our lives would change dramatically over the years. This leaving felt like a painful cutting of the cord, and ever since Anna had died, I'd absolutely hated goodbyes, as I do to this day. They'd started a small collection of money as a going-away present, Carol sticking an envelope in my hand from all of them. Mary gave me a hug and put her brown silk Hermès scarf, still smelling like the Diva perfume she wore, over my shoulders. 'You'll need something nice in California to start your collection,' she said with a wink. And I was off, pushed with so much love and strength and determination that I could almost feel it as a gust of warm wind at my back as I drove away.

I picked Bill up early in the morning, he travelling lightly with nothing more than a backpack and a Gypsy Kings cassette tape, which would see us through dusty towns in Texas, New Mexico, Arizona, Nevada and the deserts of California. We stayed in threadbare motels with air conditioners that smelled of cigarettes and must, Bill always taking his own room. Our miles in the car were filled with hour on hour of his stories about life when he was younger, his drinking days, his son Billy, the long road to sobriety and his great love of literature. We stopped in dusty one-horse towns, eating eggs and hash at small diners, getting sideways looks from the occasional waitress trying to figure out this unlikely pairing. We got sunburned on a Navajo reservation looking at pottery, and watched the spectacular night-time lightning storms in Arizona that Bill loved so much he would eventually move there. When we finally arrived in Los Angeles, we found my apartment building easily, but Bill wouldn't let me drive him on to Bukowski's house in San Pedro because he was afraid I would get lost. He briefly met my roommates and called himself a cab, leaving with as little fanfare as when he'd decided to take the journey with me. I'd spent a total of ten days driving across the country with Bill and heard enough of his story to know that he too hated goodbyes.

*

My apartment was in a wooden building on a street called Bridewell. My roommates were Rachel and two other summer messengers, Kathleen and Dru. The apartment had two beds in the only bedroom and two futons in the living room. Dru was rarely around because she was dating a sportswriter who lived in Marina Del Rey, and Kathleen frequently stayed at her family's place nearby in a town called Eagle Rock. I liked all three of them, especially Kathleen, who came from an Irish family and was hysterically funny in her bluntness and enthusiasm about everything. Living with others came easily having shared already in Indianapolis; it felt like an effortless transition.

But nothing could have prepared me for the *Los Angeles Times*, a newspaper that took up an entire city block of downtown Los Angeles, and from whose balcony you could look down to Parker Center, the police headquarters that I knew at first sight because it was the centrepiece shot of every 1970s police drama ever made. Inside was gigantic and overwhelming, and absolutely pulsing with activity: twelve hundred journalists and editors in desk groups called pods, the paper sectioned off into different areas, from Business to Metro to Sports, Foreign, National and everything else. There was a well-stocked kitchen that the food section used to test recipes, and the photo area still had dark rooms. As a copy messenger, my job was to deliver faxes and retrieve research and pictures from the library, as well as traverse almost all of downtown Los Angeles and its various buildings, picking up documents and delivering them from the Hall of Administration, the criminal courts and City Hall. I walked so much during my first month that I lost fifteen pounds. At night I had to cut out articles from the paper selected by the Washington bureau chief, paste them on paper and fax them to the White House, because before the Internet, the president would get a briefing book of all the top news of the day contributed by every major paper. If you worked the late shift, you might be lucky enough to get the Coffey run, which meant taking an editorial car to deliver the first edition of the paper, fresh off the press, to the home of the editor-in-chief, Shelby Coffey.

The best times at the paper were when a big story was happening, and there were many. During the Oscars, photographers would need to dress in tuxes and full evening gowns to shoot the event, with runners on motorcycles ready to catch spent rolls of film from the working photographers and drive off with them at breakneck speed to the paper so they could be developed. Operation Desert Storm riveted the newsroom, with TVs everywhere tuned to CNN – this was the first war ever to have live television coverage. There was the stunning announcement that Magic Johnson, the beloved LA Lakers point guard, had HIV, his press conference bringing everyone in the massive newsroom to a complete standstill, silent with shock at the news, and then snapping into action to cover the story. The paper had twenty-six foreign bureaus around the world, one of the largest foreign news operations on earth. The paper was, at the time, regarded as one of the top two papers in the United States – along with the *New York Times* – and the energy of the newsroom was palpable.

I came to know George Cotliar, the paper's managing editor, quickly. Cotliar had approved me for the summer messenger job, and I took a shine to him immediately; he was avuncular in every way. He sat in a glass-walled office at the corner of the newsroom – at the intersection of the Metro and National sections – and his office was always full of editors coming and going, proofs of stories in hand. Cotliar was beloved by nearly everyone. The messengers were generally in his remit, and he was naturally good-natured but didn't suffer fools if you made a mistake or wasted his time on deadline. I came to love having to drop things into his office and saying hello, as he looked up from marking stories with a red grease pen. He'd always asked me how I was getting along at the paper and in general. He became more and more like a father figure to me, because he knew I'd come from Indiana alone, and he had a daughter just slightly older than I was.

I loved the *Times* so much that I could have been locked in at the paper twenty-four hours a day working and I would have been thrilled. The editors and reporters fascinated me and I regarded most of them with reverence, spending hours poring over their articles, learning as I went along – how to use reverse directories, organized by address, to find phone numbers, or how to interpret the codes on police scanners from one of the newspaper's greatest characters, the overnight city editor Nieson Himmel, a living encyclopaedia of Los Angeles crime stories dating back to the Black Dahlia, a story on which he reported. Nieson was a gigantic man who wore Havana shirts and had a desk covered with so many stacks of paper that you could barely see his balding head over the top of them as he sat with eyes half-closed, lightly dozing, while listening to the police and fire scanners, giving the paper a head start on stories again and again.

The City desk was one of the busiest parts of the paper, and soon I was assigned to the coveted messenger job there, reading news alerts for stories and sharing them with the city editors over short messages sent through a computer system called the Coyote. The job also involved opening huge and endless volumes of mail, reviewing press releases and directing them to the correct reporter, and answering calls from the general public. The calls were diverse, challenging and entertaining, from a woman who called to say she had a bird's nest stuck in her ear to people who needed the paper to expose injustices, from illegal hiring practices to bum landlords. Learning to handle these calls took skill and there was a steep learning curve at the beginning: on deadline, the editors' time was sacrosanct, and you never wanted to put through a call without a very, very good reason. I learned the hard way when a call came in from a very authoritative voice for a city editor named Welkos – the caller wanting to know if Welkos was in the building because it was an urgent matter. 'Yes, he's here but he's busy, can I put you on hold?' Welkos went ballistic. He'd violated a gag order from a judge by allowing a reporter to write about a court proceeding, and because he was in contempt of the order, they were looking to come and arrest him. I'd inadvertently tipped off the bailiff and Welkos was afraid he'd have to stay in a hotel for a few days and hide until things blew over.

I loved the paper, not only for the energy and the excitement, but because everyone was so welcoming and encouraging. Maybe it was because I was young or because I was an utterly non-threatening blonde girl from Indiana who was so unsophisticated that I pronounced 'tortilla' with two *l*'s instead of a *y*. Beyond a few dismissive and gruff editors, straight from central casting, who were equally unpleasant to everyone, it felt as if I was developing a giant family of interesting people. I couldn't wait to come to work every day, bounding through the sections of the paper, dropping off documents and library research, chatting with anyone that would talk with me. I was in an educational nirvana, made even better because the intensity of the environment and the shared task of turning out a paper every day inspired camaraderie. I wanted to be like these people, and I wanted to write.

I had always been quirky, so much so that I never saw it as an asset, and wasn't consciously aware that my childhood had made me naturally gravitate to people and ideas that were somehow offbeat or *other* because that's where I felt most at home. I didn't know it when I started thinking up story ideas, but, at eighteen years old, I was the youngest person in the newsroom, and by virtue of my age alone, I had a different perspective. At the time there was a Metro column called Cityscapes, featuring slices of life in LA, and I became obsessed with the idea of writing for it. One day, one of the editors who oversaw assignments for the column decided to give me a chance. I can't remember what story I wrote first, but they poured out of me: a column on the life of Dainty Adore O'Hara, a transvestite punk rock opera singer in Hollywood; a profile of Curley Alba Morrow, a septuagenarian from Oklahoma who lived in the back room of a trendy art gallery on Melrose, cleaning up the place and drinking Schlitz beer and reading Louis L'Amour novels in his off time, inspiring a world of artists in the process. I once stayed overnight at Canter's, a twenty-four-hour deli on Fairfax Avenue, to see who on earth would be eating corned beef on rye at 3 a.m. I spent another night in an emergency call centre in a bunker underneath City Hall, listening to harrowing calls come in from kids whose parents were having drug overdoses and even one parent who'd been shot. And with every story I wrote, the editors would sit with me and edit, carefully explaining why they were moving a paragraph here or there, or why I needed to 'tighten the lede' – the opening paragraph meant to get to the heart of the story economically.

*

The paper was all-consuming, but I needed to think about college. As far as I could see, my only options were the state university, UCLA, which was enormously expensive for out-of-state students and far from the paper, a job I couldn't and didn't want to quit. The University of Southern California was just a mile from the newspaper, making it possible to continue working there, and it had a fantastic journalism programme. It was also one of the most expensive private universities in the United States, and although my father was continuing to help me financially, I knew there was no way they would agree to the tuition at USC.

A solution came unexpectedly, suggested by one of my roommates. I could take the next year of college courses at a junior college – a respectable two-year college that was practically free. I'd knock out most of my general credits and could then apply to USC and finish out my two years there when I decided on a major, working full-time and taking out student loans to help cover the tuition. When the time came, I was accepted into USC and planned to major in journalism – until Cotliar, who'd become even more of an advisor, stopped me from doing so. 'You're learning to write here at the paper,' he pointed out. 'Major in something that will tell you more about the world, like political science.' It became my major.

I only came back to Indiana a couple of times, and the visits were frosty and formal. I loved my dad, and he took great interest in the work I was doing, frequently sending me encouraging typewritten letters, cartoons from the *New Yorker* and articles he'd cut out from the *Wall Street Journal*. He continued to help me financially because I was in college. I knew he was proud of me and it meant everything to have his approval, but coming home, I always had the sense that I'd done something wrong and wasn't welcome. Joan had never put pictures up of any of the Galloway kids, and I noticed that a gift I'd given them – a black and white photo I'd had taken by a *Times* photographer and put in a silver frame – had been unceremoniously relegated to a storage cube in a closet. It seemed the greater the exuberance with which I shared everything I was experiencing in California, the greater the dourness and rejection. No matter how much my confidence had grown in California, coming home – if you could call it that – made me feel tight in the chest and full of anxiety. I usually flew back to California in tears, grateful to be away from such a hateful atmosphere.

I learned to make the rejection an adventure. On my first Thanksgiving in California, alone, at eighteen I was too young to gamble or drink, but I'd always wanted to see Las Vegas, so I drove there on my own, spending Thanksgiving Day in a thirty-nine-dollar hotel room at The Strip, in a blue *National Velvet* themed room, eating turkey and stuffing from a room-service tray, Mickey Rooney and Elizabeth Taylor staring down at me.

One day a call came to the paper's messenger room – help was needed in the publisher's suite, where the editor-in-chief, Shelby Coffey, worked. Shelby was southern and had come from the *Washington Post* Style section, where he was the editor during the heyday of legendary publisher Kay Graham. Shelby was very much the public face of the paper: meeting with foreign dignitaries, political leaders and newsmakers; making big decisions about the paper's direction and its twelve-hundred-person newsroom. He had little time for small talk, because he had a lot to do and he was *laser focused*. I was terrified of Shelby, who was the opposite of the avuncular Cotliar. Shelby wasn't unkind, not at all. He just moved with a distanced air of purpose. He was so busy that he had two assistants, both called Linda. Assistant one was a stern woman in her fifties whose background gave her a unique trifecta for tolerating absolutely no bullshit: she was Mormon, had been a single mother for several years, raising three boys, and was a former LAPD officer. She could reduce you to ashes with one stern look of disapproval, no words needed. Assistant two, Linda Ko, followed everything the other Linda directed her to do. But things were busy, and the Lindas needed a third person to sub in, so it was decided that that person would be me for a few days a week, when I wasn't on the City desk.

My work started with sorting the hundreds of letters that came in to Shelby, deciding which he needed to answer, which needed to go to different editorial departments and which should be discarded. It was a full-time job, and this is partially why three assistants were necessary – Linda One was focused on scheduling and other confidential newspaper matters.

Long before the days of satnav, I was also given the job of typing out directions to the various locations Shelby had to travel for meetings and dinners, using a map directory book of southern California called the *Thomas Guide*. I hated this task more than anything because I was the most directionally challenged person on earth, even with a detailed map, and having to figure out and type directions for one of the most important people in Los Angeles gave me heart palpitations; I lived in fear of accidentally sending Shelby to Cerritos when he really should have been in Beverly Hills with a famous studio head or titan of business.

Every afternoon, Shelby would at some point come into the publisher's suite and stand in front of the three of us assistants, quickly going through folders of letters that needed responses, yeses or nos to invitations and meetings to be scheduled. I was a fast typist and eventually I was tasked with dictating Shelby's response letters, which were an extraordinary education in, well, everything. I learned from Shelby the art of advanced vocabulary to get a point across in an elegant (or biting) way; I learned the word *retromingent*; I learned about poets like Rudyard Kipling (he quoted the poem *If* frequently) and NWA, whom, inexplicably, he could also quote at length, as if reciting Tennyson. I was afraid of Shelby, in awe of his importance and his seriousness – so afraid that one day, when he came in to go through his folders, desperate not to interrupt or call attention to myself, my bladder about to burst, I literally peed my pants while sitting at my desk.

Shortly after I'd graduated from college, I wanted to apply for a reporter's position in the San Fernando Valley bureau, an outpost of the paper. But I'd also been offered a job editing a new website started by a *Times* business editor who'd left. Shelby quietly suggested that I take the job with the editor, leaving the *Times*. I was crushed, believing that Shelby did not think I was good enough to become a full-time staff writer.

When I told everyone I was leaving, Shelby and Cotliar jointly threw a going-away party for me at an upscale hotel nearby, inviting all of the editors and reporters with whom I'd worked and grown up. The Supercuts women had given me safety and strength and the gumption to go out in the world; the people at the paper had opened it up for me, setting the rhythm for things that I would care about in my professional life, shaping me. They also looked out for me, as friends, as mentors. The paper had become a loving family for me, just as the women of

Supercuts had. My dad wrote Cotliar a letter, thanking him for being a father figure to me.

It wasn't until much later that I learned that Shelby had advised me not to take the job at the paper because a round of lay-offs was imminent, and the new job would have meant I would have been one of the first to be let go. He couldn't tell me at the time. And it was Shelby who would be there for me many years later, changing from a venerated boss to a friend and confidant, as life unfolded in Norway.

9

ALONE

Áilu is gone. He leaves in the night in early February, the dead of winter, when the temperature is minus thirty degrees. I don't have a cell phone, so he sends me a simple message on Facebook. He's moving back to his mother and father's house, half a kilometre away, the only steady home he has known in his semi-nomadic life as a reindeer herder. He is matter-of-fact: he doesn't want to be with me any more; he is going to the mountain to look after his herd; I need to move. 'Go back to New York,' he tells me. He is efficient and swift in his delivery, much the same way he might kill a reindeer.

I did not see this coming. Not nearly. We have just spent a happy New Year's together. As part of my annual New Year's tradition, I've just written in my journal about things for which I am grateful in the previous year, alongside my hopes and aspirations for the coming one: I will learn to knit, I will master Sámi, I will get my snowmobile licence. But now everything unravels in an instant, and nothing makes sense.

Where were the signs? What happened? I struggle to understand. The last time we spent time together, we visited his sister early on New Year's evening and watched King Harald's annual holiday address on NRK in her living room, then drank Isbjorn beers with friends in the local pub well into the night, laughing and merry making, taking selfies. Soon after that, he departed for the mountain and has been gone for several weeks with virtually no contact, which is common. Áilu is always away for indeterminate lengths of time.

The message blindsides me, shaking me to the core in a way that is physical and ancient, going back to other moments in which I'd felt all stability evaporate and the earth crumble: when my mother had died suddenly or when my marriage with Richard had ended. The depth of my brokenness and shame comes out geyser-like in moments like this; a primal fear of abandonment manifesting itself in deep despair to the point of becoming frozen and in a state of shock, made worse here because I am in a place where I really know nothing about managing daily life on my own.

The shock of the announcement is compounded by my shame in wondering if I have completely miscalculated my level of inclusion. Who did I think I was, believing that this family would have anything to do with me? I have wrongly believed I'd fallen into a type of comfortable rhythm, a level of acceptance, even, and was starting to imagine a future in Kautokeino. While Áilu was away during the holidays, I spent Christmas Eve with his mother and father, sisters and brothers at the family home, where children of all ages squealed with the giddy delight of the season and tore through the well-worn house, wild with the joy of seeing cousins and family and all of the presents and games. Áilu's mother, Inger Marit, as is the custom with most *áhkut*, or grandmothers, was wearing her traditional *gákti*, and we took pictures for me to send home to my friends. Everyone was in a cheery mood; even Áilu's father, Johan, who speaks no English, managed to break from his normal scowl and smile at me as he sat in his wheelchair and smoked his rolled cigarettes at the kitchen stove. There were more than twenty of us, and we ate *risgrøt*, Norwegian Christmas rice pudding, while sitting on a mishmash of mismatched tables and chairs covered with festive holiday oilcloths. The serving of the *risgrøt* centred around the tradition of hoping to be served the lucky ladleful that contained the single almond mixed in with the batch, affording the recipient a small prize, usually a bar of chocolate. This year, the almond was in my bowl. It was going to be my year.

I was mesmerized and delighted at being pulled into this family's chaotic fold, even if I couldn't understand half of what was being said. It was such an enormous difference from my own solitary and emotionally tepid childhood in Indiana, where noise, acting out or any expressions of joy were met with threat and rejection. And this is why losing Áilu also feels like losing an entire family, a shock and realization that doesn't come for most people until much later in a break-up – but I had come to feel that I was as much joining a family as a partner, reinforced by the fact that here, in a culture in which family historically meant not only blood relation but literally being tied to a group for survival, being with a partner really did mean joining the entire family more than in many other cultures.

Having just spent the holidays with everyone, and in growing despair, this loss is at the top of my mind, sitting alongside the break-up with an equal amount of grief. Especially the loss of Áilu's mother, Inger Marit. From the start, she treated me with a softness and openness that showed itself through her eyes, transcending our language barrier. She patiently taught me how to do *gámasneaskin*. She always nodded her head encouragingly, saying *'juo, juo, juo'* (yes, yes, yes) as if she understood every broken word I spoke when I struggled to speak Sámi, even when I was accidentally insulting her curtains. I admired her tireless work ethic and the care she took with managing the family: baking loaf after loaf of bread every day, even though there are now two grocery stores in town. Each morning and evening she'd put on her boots and go out to feed any number of reindeer that might be in their yard, getting fattened up to safely return to the tundra. She was always in a state of motion: sewing *gákti* or cutting wood or doing other essential work, all usually with grandchildren in tow. She was always in the fence when the reindeer were gathered for counting or slaughter, working alongside everyone, even if for days on end. That was the way. Inger Marit is a whisper in my heart of the women from which I came – my great-grandmother, my grandmother and mother – but was scarcely able to know, and for this reason I feel a strong connection to her that I will now be losing.

In particular, Inger Marit reminds me so much of my own maternal grandmother, Grammie, in both looks and temperament that often when I watched her milling about her chores I'd find myself with a lump in my throat. Both were wisps of women, no strangers to backbreaking work and heartache and soldiering on because it is the only way. For Grammie it was losing her parents in the devastating influenza epidemic of 1918 and being put out to work as a maid along with my great-aunt Ellen when both were less than fourteen years of age, then facing a constant stream of unimaginable loss as an adult: losing her only daughter, my mother, and then Anna, to whom she was extraordinarily close, and then her husband. For Inger Marit it was raising eight children, one of whom was killed in a snowmobile accident, caring for a husband paralysed in a terrible car accident, surviving through bad herding years, ups and downs in money and grief.

With Áilu away, the normal steps in a break-up like talking it out and trying to understand what led to this aren't possible. Even lashing out isn't possible. My mind races in circles, trying to grasp it all. The more I think about the holidays that just passed, the more I come back to one evening in particular, Christmas night, when Áilu's sister had invited me to the home of her in-laws, several kilometres away in a part of Kautokeino called Ávži. The matriarch of the family, Ruhte, was a very traditional Sámi woman whom I'd met once before, at a Christening party for a baby in the family. Ruhte spoke very clear and solid English, but would not use it with me previously, as I was learning Sámi. But on Christmas night, she'd looked me dead in the eye and asked in perfect English, with what I believed to be an admonishment as much as a question: 'Why haven't you gone to be with Áilu and the reindeer?' I realized only in retrospect that I'd made a giant mistake by not joining him – at the time, I thought I'd be a hindrance if he needed to move fast or a difficulty arose. That, and he never knew when he was coming back, which inspired impossible anxiety in me about who would watch the cats or what would happen if we were gone for a long period of time from our apartment that needed the heat of a hand-stoked fire to make it liveable for any creature.

At the time, it didn't seem to bother him much that I wasn't going, because he'd only asked once, and limply, and he never liked participating in family gatherings so was eager to get away. I knew that Áilu was a man of few words: both a function of his culture and his personality. He liked to be alone with his thoughts and his animals. And so I also reasoned that I was respecting his space. To celebrate the holidays, I believed I'd adequately shown my affection by hiding in his sledge of supplies some Christmas presents to occupy him at the family's winter place where he'd be based: thick socks, car magazines, a few of the lotto scratcher tickets to which he was addicted and a six-pack of Isbjorns. But I am slowly understanding that not joining him showed a deficit of the dedication expected of a partner of a herder. We had no children to manage, and I should have gone with him to keep him company, to work. This is something bigger than that moment in particular. It illustrates the weight of the differences between our cultures, which it is now clear, is a weight that is too much. At its core, the issue is our competing ideas of home: his the mountains; mine a state of mind and not a place.

Now I am on my own, unsure of how to handle everything. Kautokeino is a place where everything is still largely unknown to me, from practicalities to the cultural norms, both previously viewed through the lens of Áilu and what he'd share. If I am to stay, I'll need to move forward with a new and steep learning curve ahead of me.

My first inclination is to get under the covers and never wake up because it's all too overwhelming. But with Áilu abruptly gone, there is little time to feel sorry for myself. I of course make sobbing calls to close friends but am then forced to stop the self-indulgence and sort out the many details that Áilu had taken care of previously. Where to pay rent. How to pay the Internet bill. Where to get firewood, which I rely on to heat our freezing cold apartment. I am suddenly aware that I don't know how to do any of these things.

I feel I have no family to turn to; it's largely been my friends who know me best and who are there for me in a crisis, so I spend much of my time talking through what I might do with my friends Adam and Deb in the US. As well-intentioned and supportive as their advice may be, the realities of life here don't match any advice that they offer, and it always ends the same way: 'Come home.' It is sensible advice. It is also advice I cannot heed. Deep in my core, I know that it is not time to run or retreat, to pack up and leave. That would be easy and weak. I've been accommodating others' abrupt and unpredictable behaviour my entire life, slinking out of situations, calling defeat, letting shame and loneliness eat at me like a ravenous worm through an orchard apple until I'd almost lost myself entirely – precisely the reasons I'd given up on New York.

It will not happen again. I've invested so much here – leaving behind the life I knew, learning the language, dragging my cats halfway across the world. There is also that old chestnut called pride. I still have some, plus a surfeit of experience in one life skill: navigating ambiguity. And there is the land – something about this place has taken root inside of me, holding me, telling me it is not time to leave. I cannot look back.

Áilu sends me another message telling me that I'll need to leave the apartment, even though I've been paying rent. This is because the lease is in his name. Of all the things I have to figure out here, I'm by far the most terrified about this problem, because it's the dead of winter and there is a housing shortage in the village, this much I know. There is a long line of people who would want the apartment. I have no idea where I'd even go if I needed to move, or where to look. Áilu also informs me that there is a deposit on the apartment, which he demands back if I try to stay. I am starting to wonder if this break-up was also about money.

I message Áilu's sister Rávdná on Facebook – she helps me with the name of the apartment manager and then says she can't help more. 'Áilu is my brother,' she explains. 'I want to help you, but I cannot go against him.' And there is simply no more contact, confusing me more and making me wonder why any side needs to be taken at all. And what is Áilu saying to his family? What do they think? We hadn't had an argument and I wasn't asking her to belittle her brother, only for some help in unravelling what I must do next. But I will come to learn that this reaction is not at all exclusive or particular to me; once you are out of the family, you are out completely, no matter the circumstance.

At the same time as the break-up, I'm also in the second semester of my first year of gruelling and complicated Sámi language study at the university. The first courses had been geared towards beginning learners, and no intermediate classes were available before the next level, so I found myself in a class with primarily native Sámi speakers coming mostly to shore up their grammar. I am completely over my head, barely able to keep up with the class and now utterly distracted with basic life navigation rather than noun conjugations.

It is my old Sámi teacher, a very kind-hearted woman named Marja, in whom I first confide about my situation. She thought I was amusing when I was her student, and we always exchange friendly hellos when I see her around the university. Marja is Sámi from the Swedish side and married a herder from Kautokeino, so she knows what it means to be from another place without connection to some degree. I've been completely alone and all of my emotions pour out at the sight of a friendly face. I burst into tears and explain to her the situation with the apartment, and that I am afraid of losing it and don't know how to fix the problem. I've since been told that Áilu had cancelled the lease altogether, and I understood that I would not be able to have the lease transferred to me because of the many people who are waiting for housing. The head of the kommune rental company speaks Sámi primarily, and then Norwegian and no English. There would be no way to make my case or ask for them to make an exception. The apartment administration office is just down the hill from the university, and Marja makes a plan: we will go at lunchtime and she will speak to him.

When we go to the office, Marja speaks quickly as the man listens. I'm so worried that I burst into tears in front of him again. If you are Sámi or Norwegian, these displays of emotion just don't happen. I don't know if it is embarrassment, or confusion, or just plain kindness that motivated Odd Ole on that day, but he decides to sign the apartment over to me, and I no longer have to worry about where I will live.

As anyone who has ever lived in a small town or village can attest, news travels faster in these places. Kautokeino is no different. Idle gossip and whispers abound. Most of the village is already clucking about the break-up. I see it in the way people look at me as I walk through town or visit the market. I have no one here to confide in. But Stein is a couple of hours away by car. I call him and tell him what's happened, and silently and without prompting, he makes the two-hour drive up the *vidda* to my apartment in Kautokeino, where he drives me to a store for firewood, sneaks 500 kroner into my jacket pocket, and offers me work freelancing for his newspaper, even though he'll need to personally translate all of my writing from English to Norwegian. He listens to me cry, we drink red wine at my kitchen table, and he teaches me, as a newspaper editor who has heard and seen everything, what he has learned over the years about the hearts and minds of herders, as well as what I must do to survive if I am to stay in a place so far from home, in every way.

10

BROKEN

When I was younger, I was fascinated by the concept of nervous breakdowns – the physical manifestations of them, to be exact. What was a nervous breakdown? It was a term filled with intrigue. Here and there, on dramatic seventies TV programmes, or occasionally in whispered adult gossip, you'd hear the phrase 'he or she had a nervous breakdown' tossed around as if it was something profound and shameful, a delicious secret which I imagined to involve going completely and utterly insane, running naked down the street screaming or banging one's head against a concrete wall in a fit of wild emotion. Joan would always say, with an air of judgement, that her first husband, Phil, had a nervous breakdown, something that confounded me as a little girl because I'd met him once or twice during events like my stepsister Jane's graduation, and could find no evidence of this; he appeared perfectly kind and normal, with clean clothing and well-combed hair. I always wondered precisely how one went about having a nervous breakdown, so I would be ready were one ever to happen to me, or so if I saw someone having one on the street, I could help, just as I would endeavour to help someone having a heart attack or a seizure.

These were the sorts of concerns that swirled in my childhood brain. And then you grow up and mysteries are solved with age and experience, like knowledge of various clinical psychological conditions because of the people you will come to know who have or will develop them. During college, I had a good friend and neighbour in Los Angeles who would do things like knock manically at my door at midnight suggesting drives to Palm Springs or going across town to eat potato knishes at Canter's deli at three in the morning. These adventures, and I found them to be just that at the time, still in my late teens, were inevitably followed by my friend crashing and burning in spectacular fashion, the mania bookended by major fits of depression in which she didn't have the energy to even call in sick to work, or to eat, or to change clothes, or to wash for days and sometimes weeks on end, with no external solution in sight; it was as if there was something unreachable inside of her that could not be altered or set right. The invention of Prozac ultimately helped my friend, whom I would come to understand had what was clinically referred to as manic depression. But the only language I had for it then was 'nervous breakdown', because I did not know what it meant.

And then, in New York, having just turned forty, I started to wonder if I was, in fact, having a nervous breakdown, because I simply had no language to articulate how in one moment you can be on top of the world, holding everything together, gorgeous, in a beautiful apartment and with one of the best jobs in the world, and then a string is abruptly pulled and the whole tapestry, the whole life you've constructed for yourself, starts to unravel. It doesn't happen at one moment, but slowly: one thread comes loose and it's only a matter of time until so too do all the warps and wefts that make the whole; the picture you had woven for yourself is frayed and coming apart and it is all too complicated to fix; everything has become tangled to the point of chaos and too big and daunting to repair. This was the point at which I had arrived.

Although I'd mostly been alone, for the first time I was starting to feel the hollow and isolating side of what this word meant. I'd always been independent and pushed through the world solo and largely without fear. This was mostly because my greatest gift in life had been that in the absence of emotional support from a family, I'd managed to find authentic and fulfilling relationships through friends and mentors who'd acted as surrogates, like the women at Supercuts, or the people at the paper. They had pushed me onward and out into the world, giving me attention and confidence.

After leaving the *Times* and working on a couple of dot.com projects during the Wild West days of the Internet, I'd landed in New York to work for a company that went bankrupt just weeks after my arrival. I was living in a small studio in Greenwich Village, and despite my employment misfortune, I scrapped my way through this unexpected twist in the most New York fashion possible, just doing whatever I needed to do to survive – from managing a restaurant in the Village on weekends to cleaning apartments, doing Girl Friday work for a famous astrologer on Fifth Avenue, and even attempting to sell private jet flights. After the paper, I'd developed solid experience in business development and marketing, and I eventually once again found work doing this in a job with an executive recruiter who'd made a mint hiring and placing employees for a multitude of dot. com companies. She'd also written a book that needed promotion, and I was hired for both efforts. I was at the job briefly before her consultancy folded when the effects of the Internet crash came around and there were no longer companies that needed employee recruitment. It was my second abrupt lay-off in a year, so I decided to pursue an idea I'd been contemplating for some time: starting my own media strategy consultancy, focused on sharing everything I knew about shaping and communicating important ideas, working with journalists like the ones I'd admired, instead of being one of them, because the writing was clearly on the wall for the future of journalism because of the Internet. I had high aspirations for my idea: I decided that I would not handle celebrities or politicians, or work on typical public relations efforts, instead focusing on the people and ideas that I felt needed to be connected to the world. Slowly, the consultancy grew, and in a tremendous stroke of luck, or kismet, or whatever you want to call it, a former journalist friend who'd acquired a small private conference company and wanted to share it with the world, hired me to head up all of the external media relations. Three people were working for him when I started, and no one had heard of the conference, which was a non-profit, beyond an exclusive group of people who attended on the west coast every year. In the beginning, it was a challenge to find the journalists and ways to help connect the gathering to the world, but over time, it became my major client and an almost all-consuming project for a number of years; the conference grew, became international and started an online arm sharing content with the world, viewed by billions of people. I was in a unique inside-outside role: I was hired as their head of media relations while still able to run my own firm and take on other clients when there was time and bandwidth.

The conference grew wildly, beyond anyone's expectations, and I found myself travelling the world, from England to Africa to India and many places in between, meeting and working with some of the most brilliant people on earth. I loved my job beyond measure, although there were tiny fissures in the day-to-day: a hyper-competitive environment and internal jockeying that sometimes felt as if I was back in high school, everyone vying for the attention and favour of the commander-in-chief. It was worth it, and I figured this was what happened when one worked in such an intense environment.

My family was around, but distant. Ever since I'd moved to New York, with only a pause when I married Richard, I would travel up the eastern seaboard for Thanksgiving to Maine, where Dad and Joan had retired, near to my stepsister Jane and her husband, Rick, and Linda, who'd long ago divorced and was living on her own. I kept in occasional contact with my brothers via email, but I hadn't seen Mark in years and saw Will on just one brief visit, when he came to New York for a couple of days. When I went up to Maine, I'd take a bus that departed from Chinatown called the Fung Wah, which cost something like six dollars and drove at breakneck speeds, dumping passengers on the side of the freeway off-ramp adjacent to Boston's South Station, and then take the train to Maine, where everyone lived. I always stayed with Jane and Rick.

The trips always, always ended in heartbreak but I kept coming back. Nearly every visit followed the same script: Joan would hold it together for a day or two and then without notice fly into a rage, becoming cruel or saying something awful that would chip at my core, be it comments about my looks, my profession or the Galloways in general and how we were all *pieces of work*. Jane and Rick, who'd been seeing this happen since I was small, were sympathetic privately but remained neutral. 'You're a Galloway, and Joan just hates the Galloway kids, and that's the way it is,' Rick would say after one of Joan's room-silencing outbursts, as plainly as if talking about the weather, before switching topics. 'Jane and Linda are her daughters, and you're not – blood is thicker than water,' he'd say matter-of-factly. After years of writing me long and imploring emails, and spending hours on the phone telling me that for my mental health I should abandon my parents completely, as she had done herself for a long stretch, Linda had now completely changed her tune, and my parents were back in the picture. I would be lying if I said I did not think it had something to do with money, and the fact that my father had a lot of it. The Galloway kids were desperate to see my father and be a part of his life, but my brothers rarely if ever visited. Will came occasionally, but he would fare much worse than I did on those trips, which always degenerated into Joan more or less telling him he was a piece of shit, or calling him gay because he was single and never brought girlfriends around, or accusing him of having a gambling problem, solely based on the fact that he lived in Las Vegas. His trips were always calculated to last two days or less, to avoid 'stirring the pot' as we would say. One year, Will arranged to have photos taken of himself with my dad and his beloved dog. Joan went crazy, demanding that her dog not be in pictures with my brother. These trips killed my brother a little each time because he so wanted to have contact with my father.

This treatment, and this way of being, had become normal to us – normal because the behaviour was accepted by everyone around us: no one intervened or put their foot down. When this happens, repeatedly and over years, you begin to believe the stories you are told about yourself, and ours was that we were not worthy of defence or acceptance. This was the greatest hurdle in my life – not believing those stories and prevailing over my shame. It was all the more complicated because we loved our father deeply, yet he reconciled everything that was happening and tried to manage it, rather than stand up to it or simply walk away. Why he stayed will likely remain the central question of our lives. Despite everything, our father was never directly cruel to us in even the remotest sense; he was a kind person who looked after us when our mother died; he'd always shown concern and love for us directly. It just seemed to be voided or trumped by Joan's behaviour, her fits, her eclipsing of anything else in her orbit. Her anger could swallow the sun.

I wondered at times if my dad was afraid to leave because of what might happen to Joan; it seemed as if she wouldn't be able to survive on her own, and maybe this is why he stayed. I like to think it was essentially an act of love and sacrifice, borne out of compassion. Or maybe over time he just became reconciled to this as his life. And then there was always the most difficult possibility to bear: that he'd simply chosen to be with her, despite it all. It seemed we'd never know, but nonetheless, we continued to love our father. He was, at this point, the only flesh and blood we had left.

Dramatic as it was at times, life in New York had unfolded in wonderful ways. After much heartbreak, I'd survived my divorce from Richard and was moving on. I was working constantly and travelling. Understanding that it was unlikely that I'd ever have kids of my own, I became qualified to volunteer at the New York Foundling Hospital, an orphanage that had a unit called the Crisis Nursery, where parents could leave their kids for the short term if they were unable to care for them, a stop-gap measure to avoid kids being placed into the foster system if their families were facing only temporary problems. I felt a connection to these kids and empathized with the fear they must have felt. The Foundling was just a block from my house, and I relished going over to hold the babies or tuck the kids in at night, or going on outings to McDonald's and walks around the city. Increasingly, it was also a respite from work, which I still loved, but which was becoming competitive and exclusionary. I'd spend my free time at the Foundling, and started travelling to the Arctic on vacations, captivated by the lack of cell signal and pure white space. The Foundling gave me time to feel connection; the Arctic gave me time to think and clear my head.

My major client had become a global sensation, and I was working all the time at the expense of other clients and projects for my own consultancy. I loved the work and knowing that I'd been part of helping something important grow and flourish in the world. This client had become in many ways my life and my identity, in that it was also a community of people with whom I spent most of my time and shared the same ideals and outlook. The company had grown by leaps and bounds, and while unexpected, it was not a complete shock when my friend the CEO told me that some of the executive team believed they needed a bigger firm than my three-person consultancy to handle what had grown into a major international brand. Over a couple of months, we discussed possible alternatives, from me coming on board as an employee to leaving entirely, but the internal work environment was so toxic – in part because of one power-hungry employee who held considerable sway – that I knew the former idea would never work and so I dropped it and let go. I accepted the transition, but it was one of the major changes of my life; after more than five years, I was leaving the project that was at the centre of something I was still passionate about and also at the zeitgeist of the culture. I left on good terms, but I was no longer on the inside and had not yet been faced with the reality to come: that many of the people in my orbit had only been there because I was in a position of influence. When I left my job, it was as if some of my value had also departed.

I also wasn't adequately prepared to transition. My business suffered and I was forced to lay off employees within months; this was my fault for not planning better and not looking far enough into the future or anticipating negative outcomes. I simply could not bring in business fast enough, and everything seemed to be crumbling around me. I was in a perpetual state of crippling stress and fear; I felt there was nowhere to go and no one in whom to confide; I felt I had to put on a brave face because who would want to help someone who was losing in such a big way? A casual drinker before, I now started drinking every night, and way too much. It blunted the pain and turned things off for me, including my sense of morality and reason. Clinging to my old life, I started having an affair with a married man I'd met through work. He was never with his wife and travelled constantly – they seemed to be together as a function of wealth preservation and keeping up a public face, although I'll never know. I justified my terrible behaviour by telling myself that this was the way the world actually worked: it had been done to me, and so fuck it. I felt an insatiable aloneness, and the irony was that the affair just denigrated my sense of self even further – with him flying into New York or whatever city we both happened to be in, tossing rolls of cash on the bed before he left to cover the cost of the hotels in which we'd always meet. This was a man who was a champion of women's rights and gender equality and minorities, and he was lauded for these things in his working life. Yet here we were.

At exactly the same time, my father had taken a bad fall and was in the hospital. No one told the Galloways. We found out only days later. Jane and Linda commandeered my father's care, neglecting to apprise us of what was happening. Rick, knowing this was wrong, sometimes secretly called to update me, and I learned from him that they'd listed themselves as my father's daughters in the hospital records, failing to mention my existence or include my contact information, even though I was an hour away by plane and had often expressed my desire to help. It felt as if the Galloways were now being pushed out of a relationship with our father, the last person we had left. My territorial instincts went into overdrive. I lashed out at Jane and stopped talking to Linda for what I saw as her complete hypocrisy – for so long aggressively encouraging division in the family and then moving in to assume a position in which she controlled everything, and he wasn't even her father. I called Joan and said I wanted to visit my dad; this was unsurprisingly met with hysterics and an insistence on no Galloways. My dad, now in his early eighties, wasn't reachable by phone. It felt as if everything that mattered had been taken from me and was evaporating before my eyes.

The affair ended on the worst night of my life. I'd had wine and taken Ambien, the medication that makes one sleep, and in my case, apparently, hallucinate. I texted the man with whom I was having an affair that I was going to end my life. This was medication and booze talking, not me; as low as I've ever been, I've never considered suicide an option, believing that earth is a school and you just have to wade your way through it, no matter what. My text was answered by a group of paramedics banging at my door, insisting that I go to the hospital for a psychiatric evaluation. I sat next to a college student jacked up on Adderall, knees clacking and in tears because she thought she was going to miss a test the next day. I wondered how it had all come to this. Was this a nervous breakdown, the thing I'd wondered about my entire life? After a couple of hours of waiting, I was evaluated, and I'd also sobered up. The doctor asked me a series of questions and wanted to know if there was anyone they could call to discuss my general state of mind. I gave them the phone number of Adam, one of my best friends who lives in Los Angeles. He told the doctor I was fine, just under unprecedented stress: money stress, work stress, my family and my personal life. And they let me go.

Aside from the shame, there were things I knew I needed to fix. I knew that the life I was living did not serve me: my fast-paced, endlessly climbing, materially focused life; the friends that weren't there when it was going off the rails; people who were around only as long as I had a utility and a purpose. I'd played an active part in this dynamic: the illusion of relevance and my deep need to be accepted. I spent months contemplating what to do next, and it kept coming back to one thing. The only place I felt safety and refuge and inspiration was the Arctic. I needed a radical departure from everything I knew. And then there was Áilu. The north called. I was going.

11

ANGELS APPEAR

Aside from school and grocery shopping, I leave my apartment rarely; I have no car, and there is no one to give me rides if I did want to go anywhere. There is a small local market, one room, called the COOP in the centre of the village, just above the hardware store, but it's so small that it often doesn't have the things I need, like bags of heavy cat litter. Those I can only get from the bigger chain store, Rema 1000, which sits at the opposite side of the village, a short distance by car but what feels like miles when carrying the heavy bags in the frigid cold up the hill that defines the centre of Kautokeino, the outline of my breath heaving out from me like cartoon thought bubbles, frosty and flat and hanging in the air, trailing behind me.

The line between days and nights is faded here. Polar night in the Arctic extends from November to January, when the sun is completely absent, which at first is both novel and magical, but the feeling is also disorienting and gives daily life an unsettling and rudderless quality. I never considered how important the sun was in setting a rhythm to life until it was gone completely. Now it is slowly coming back, but it still remains dark from very early in the afternoon until late in the morning, leaving hours and hours spent inside and activating something primal that leads me to eat anything and everything, from loaves of cheap bread with butter to heavy stews with strange cuts of discounted meat that I dig out of the freezer section at the store. I spend an inordinate amount of time cooking to keep busy. I roast everything for hours: turnips, carrots, potatoes, garlic and onions. For a novice in surviving their first Arctic winter, cold and dark paired together inspire excessive carbohydrate loading. It also doesn't help that the fresh fruit and vegetables that arrive at one of the world's northernmost grocery stores generally turn up limp and tired – and wildly expensive, to boot: four pounds for a bunch of celery that had probably travelled farther than most people ever will in their lifetimes, triple sealed in plastic only to end up wilting and neglected, turgid and alone on the grocery shelf. I am gaining weight practically by the hour.

Stein is busy with his own life two hours away, and there is no one in the village for me to talk with regularly; I wish I had a nearby friend. I keep away from Áilu's family because I am beginning to understand more clearly that, culturally, if you are out of the family here, you are truly out, which is why I also can't find the courage to approach the one person I might have: Marit, Áilu's sister-in-law. Not entirely understanding the unspoken social system, everything feels tentative and I am completely unsure of myself and how to navigate. I've seen Áilu's mother once, as she was leaving the COOP, and our eyes locked. We both looked at each other sympathetically before rushing away. I wanted to hug her, but that isn't done here. I can't pretend to know what she thought, but her consoling eyes seemed to reveal that she felt badly about what had happened. I think she was also surprised that I'd not left.

If I wasn't acutely aware that I need to keep my wits about me to survive here, I am sure that old destructive habits would take over as mechanisms to cope with my aloneness. For starters, I would be drinking too much to numb my brain and escape. I would ask the doctor for a prescription for something to help me sleep, or calm me down, or help me focus, or take away the dull and aching depression that I cannot shake. I would wallow in self-pity, over and over again, an infinite loop of despair that would lead nowhere but back to the initial moment that made me feel terrible in the first place, but now coupled with a headache and usually regret. But here none of these diversions are possible. People don't talk out their problems, for better or for worse. They certainly don't go to a doctor for them, or get prescriptions for sleep meds or Valium at the local health centre, a place where locals only went if they were literally dying and possibly needed to be airlifted by helicopter to the nearest hospital in Hammerfest, five hours away. The local state-run liquor shop, Vinmopoloet, only opens at the weekend for a few short hours, putting an end to any moments of low impulse control – except for Saturdays, when I buy a bottle or two of wine.

I have to learn to be alone with myself here, which is an incredibly difficult thing to manage when all alternatives for diversion cease to exist. All of the things that served this function in my previous life have been summarily removed simply by virtue of the isolated part of the world in which I've landed. Through endless hours, I slowly start to wonder if my entire adult life, outside of work, which was also a sort of an addiction, has simply been about running away from myself, throwing things in my path that culture has told us are acceptable pursuits and even encouraged: food, Internet usage (and in particular, social media, which can be soul crushing), shopping, binge-watching TV, networking. All of these things have also kept me from my deepest self, and most of them took away from my quality of life rather than adding to it. Sitting in the cold dark of my apartment, in particular, I feel increasingly terrible looking at Facebook and Instagram, wondering how people are affording all of their incredible trips, humble-bragging about with whom they're spending time or their latest accomplishments at work, or virtue signalling with Klieg lights about the world-changing things they are doing, or their positions on politics and their attached moral outrage on a great many topics. Most of the time these things come from people who I mostly like, which makes it all the more difficult to unpack my conflicting feelings as I struggle to understand myself. It is also hard to know at times if I am simply experiencing jealousy and mourning a life that I've left behind for a future undetermined. Do I want that life again?

All of this would be easier if I had clear answers or guidance, and I wish more than anything for a life-changing epiphany or an external signal that will change my life and direction forever, but no answers come easily. I only know, and feel in my bones, that I am supposed to stay. And so I inch towards clarity. I write in my journal, and I pray – to God, and to my mom, and to Anna, and to Grammie, who are never far from my thoughts and, therefore, in some ways still alive. I pray for a friend to come; I pray for some clarity about moving forward in this new place.

I pray for a sign.

*

I've had very little interaction with Solla and Nils, my next-door neighbours, since Áilu had left, but I am getting used to a weekly routine that takes place on Fridays, when everyone gets paid. It starts in the late afternoon with the gamey and singular smell of boiled reindeer wafting through the front of the building, which would be comforting and homey as it floats into our shared entry space were it not comingled with cigarette smoke and sweat, creating a scent that, if bottled as a perfume, would most appropriately be named Despair. The cold air holds odour, and this smell seems to have particular staying power. The cooking and smoking is followed by more smoking and out-of-tune joiking (Sámi music) that gets louder and screamier as the night progresses, punctuated by the wooden front door of the apartment house slamming open and shut as drunken guests come and go, each arrival and departure shaking my bed violently because the bedroom unfortunately shares a wall with the foyer. The noise comes from all sides, as all of the windows of the apartment face the front.

One Friday, the party becomes particularly loud, and I hear Solla and Nils screaming at each other; it sounds as if she is locking him out of the building. I do a double take when I see a sofa fly in front of my living room window, then a chair and then a frying pan. I wonder if the entire contents of the apartment will be expelled before my eyes.

The fight escalates and suddenly there is screaming and pounding on my bedroom window. I can hear fists banging harder and harder at all of my windows, wild with rage, and I am terrified that Nils – and whoever else might be with him – will break in. Nils is a nice guy when sober, gentle and polite, but I've heard stories about him once drinking windshield-wiper fluid when the vodka and beers had run out. I'm certain that my windows will be broken and am aware that everyone in the village knows I'm living alone now, no longer under the protection of Áilu. I cower under the covers and decide to make a run for it, grabbing the cats and a large knife and locking myself into the bathroom, the only room in the apartment with no windows. It dawns on me that I don't even know how to call the police – what even *is* the emergency number? And so without this crucial piece of information, and my computer in the other room, I spend the night on the shower floor.

In the morning, the noise has abated, and I come out when it is light to find giant hack marks in the front door of the building, obviously made when Nils was in his rage. I momentarily consider calling the manager of the building, but then stop myself short; I don't want to be seen to be complaining and possibly risk losing the apartment that has only just been put in my hands. Outside of school, the one person I have become friendly with from my runs to the petrol station to get hot-dogs for the dogs of Kautokeino is a clerk named Bjarne, a hulking and affable Norwegian who reminds me of the Brawny Paper Towels man, a giant redheaded lumberjack used to advertise kitchen roll in America in the 1970s. Bjarne speaks perfect English and I often call him 'the mayor' because he seems to know every truck driver and the news from a six-country radius, owing to the truckers on their Arctic route who stop at the Statoil for a shower, a coffee and a chat. Bjarne has an answer for everything, and most importantly, the answers are almost always correct. He is married to a Sámi woman and knows just about every family in Kautokeino, too – everyone needs petrol. In the most general way possible, so as not to light a fuse in our gossip-prone town, I tentatively ask Bjarne what one should do if partying gets too loud or turns violent, and he enlightens me on how the local police work in the village, should I ever need them.

Nils emerges from his apartment two days later, unwashed and spent-looking. He unceremoniously greets me in Sámi while I'm out collecting the mail, as if nothing at all had happened, and for this I'm glad. But it is starting to seem sensible that I get to know my other neighbours better once the winter darkness begins to abate.

*

I struggle mightily in my Sámi language class, which has become a lost cause the further we progress in the course, deep into complicated texts and poems that I hardly understand. I learn new verbs; I try to learn the Sámi national song, *'Bures boahtin Sápmái'* (welcome to Sápmi).

I'm a slow and terrible learner, still addled by the fact that I don't speak Norwegian and there really is no way to translate what I'm reading unless I get help with explanations, which is exhausting for the person being asked. I relish going to school still, though, because of the human contact and that it gives me a focal point. I'm with an entirely new set of classmates who are mostly closer to my age or older, students who speak conversational Sámi near perfectly but want to understand the structure of the grammar better, as the way words are bent and conjugated is at the basis of the language. Everyone sees me struggle and is kind and non-judgemental, from Jan Magne, the Norwegian cafeteria chef who sometimes prepares lunches from things he's caught on the tundra or fished from the sea, to Bernt Morten, a Sámi artist who looks exactly like Richard Branson, further validating my observation that everyone on earth has a doppelganger and he or she is probably tucked away in the Arctic. I try in class, but when it all gets too far away from me, my mind wanders, and I know there's no way I will pass the challenging written and oral final exams; I weigh whether or not to drop out, but for the moment decide to hold on and absorb what I can.

The school is also a hub of activity, and one day I'm spontaneously invited by the youngest in our class, a Sámi youth activist named Marion, to take part in a protest against the dumping of mining waste in Repparfjord, a pristine Arctic fjord important to the Sámi people for fishing, and relevant to everyone in the world because of the obvious benefits of a clean ocean free of toxic mine tailings. The catalyst for the protest is Jan Tore Sanner, Norway's minister of modernization, who is visiting Kautokeino for a conference. Bernt Morten has a German girlfriend named Gerlinde who is an organizer of Idle No More Sápmi, a local chapter of an environmental justice group, and she comes to the school with a giant banner and asks me to hold one end, and we take some triumphant-looking pictures on top of a snow pile for social media as we wait for the minister, like two mountaineers planting our flag on the summit. I'm waiting for megaphones and tomatoes to arrive, and the sun is in full force and gleaming on the snow, and there is energy in the air, until the minister arrives, and I'm introduced to the urbane act of protesting, Norwegian style, which is no relation to the visibly outraged, chanting and foot-stomping protest to which I'm accustomed as an American and former New Yorker. Nordic protests are the height of civility in contrast, if this one is any measure. The minister arrives and shakes hands with the protesters, listens to them calmly make their case and responds with something tepid and non-committal in Norwegian like 'I'll have my people look into it.' And then everyone disburses and gets back to their day.

I make a mental note that I want to make friends with Gerlinde.

*

Walking home from the market one day, I'm rounding the bend home and see a woman with a long thick blonde braid and colourful yellow snow pants waving at me enthusiastically, as if summoning me. She's wearing a striped jumper and has perfect white teeth and looks like a model from a chewing-gum commercial set in the Alps rather than a person standing on a neighbourhood street in a remote Arctic village in minus twenty degrees. But most striking is that she's waving to me, as if she wants to talk to me, open and welcoming. She must have the wrong person, I think to myself, but I approach anyway.

'Hi! Are you American? I'm Stine, I wanted to say hello!' she says in absolutely perfect English, delivered with a lilting Norwegian accent. 'I know you are new here and I did want to welcome you to my house for coffee!'

I can hardly believe my ears, or my eyes. Someone is approaching me.

Stine is from the south, Fredrikstad, which accounts for her openness, which is not typically northern. Her boyfriend is a reindeer herder, with whom she has four children: three tow-headed girls aged three through eight and a darling little one-year-old boy named Mikkel Sebastian. We walk to her place, which is only a short distance from my apartment. Her home reminds me of the Norway of travel magazines and the movies: knotty pine furniture, lace curtains and warm candles. The place is simple and clean, and the embodiment of hygge, or cosy.

Stine offers me a coffee and introduces me to her girls; they mill about the dining table colouring as we chat. 'I've seen you many times and this can be a tough place,' Stine says. 'I knew that I must stop you and say hello, because I see you alone all the time.'

She is easy, light and direct, and I learn that her reindeer-herding boyfriend is often away with his herd, leaving her to care for all the children on her own, a situation that is par for the course for partners of herders, of course, except she lightly mentions that her mother-in-law isn't of much help with the children and keeps her distance from Stine. I assume it's because she's an outsider. She's studying for her master's degree in education but hasn't had time to write her thesis while raising all four kids. We make fast friends, as if we'd known each other forever.

She calls me a few days later to have coffee again and even asks me if I'll watch the smaller kids when she makes quick runs to pick the older children up from school, leaving me with little Mikkel Sebastian, who is like a doll, a rough and tumble little boy with a fixed look of determination on his face, a future reindeer herder. Stine insists on paying me when I stay with the kids, and frankly, I would do it for free but am grateful for the money. Stine may have her children, but she is also alone, and for this reason there is an unspoken connection that gradually becomes articulated. I admire how tough Stine is to move north, to a place that many southern Norwegians may never see in their lifetime, and to raise four kids here, with no knowledge of Sámi language, customs or cultures, just diving straight in. Stine gives me rides to the Rema, saving me at least one weekly backbreaking journey to and from the store with heavy cat litter. I'm delighted that I've found a friend.

I talk to Adam, my friend in Los Angeles, often, telling him about life in the Arctic in a weekly blow-by-blow, which he seems to find fascinating and weird, and I'm grateful for the connection. I rarely speak to my parents because my dad's hearing is making it more and more difficult for us to understand each other. I try to check in because that's what a good daughter does, but usually it's Joan that ends up dominating when I do call, my father somewhere in space, unable to participate. Things are fine if I stick to non-emotional matters, like describing the landscape or snow or generalities of daily life. But

I haven't spoken to them for a while, and they have no idea that I've broken up with Áilu even. I can't tell them because I knew that I would not be met with empathy or compassion, just judgement and bile from Joan, who would see it as a shortcoming of mine, rather than something that had happened to me, and wonder what I'd done to fuck up my life. She'd hated that I'd taken a DNA test to explore my ancestry, so threatened by any shadow of the past, distant or near, that she would not allow my father to take a test even for fun – she'd protested furiously to him when I suggested it and told me to never mention it again. I had to sneak a swab to him on a short visit, when she was asleep in another room. Joan thought my journey north was ridiculous, and a vague disdain always hovered in every exchange. I had learned long ago not to reveal myself to Joan, and so she really knew nothing about what had led me to leave New York, and that it had very little to do with a DNA test but everything to do with no longer feeling I had a place in the world. I had no idea who I was, only who I was supposed to be, and it all cracked open, a river of shame and hurt and confusion that needed to go upstream in order to become clear again.

I know I should tell them about Áilu, and so midway through a conversation with them I drop the news. The call shifts immediately from frigid civility to anger and venom. 'What will you do, Laura?' is Joan's response. *'And where is our money?'* When I'd started school in Norway and learned that I needed to have money on reserve in a checking account for my visa, money I didn't have at the time, I went to them for a loan, so I could show that I could support myself while studying. Now Joan has found an in to go for the jugular. And I bite back, hard. For the first time in my life, I scream back, with a rage for all the times I'd been rejected, for all the Thanksgivings alone, for all the stories I'd been made to believe about myself: that I wasn't worthy, that I was substandard, that I did not deserve happiness or safety or love. I am in heaving sobs, as everything I've wanted to say but never had the courage to comes out for the first time in forty-some years. Joan goes silent. My dad whispers, 'Laura, I insist that you don't pay that money back.'

12

BEAIVVÁŠ (SUN)

In Sápmi, there are two winters. The first winter is cold and dark, giving way to *giđđadálvi*, the second winter that bleeds into spring, when the sun makes its presence known in the most striking way possible. Under its dazzling beams everything is spectacularly, blindingly bright, reflected in cerulean skies and illuminating the whitest, purest snow for as far as the eye can see, snow that glimmers and glistens and sparkles in an ethereal perfection, weighing down giant trees and making them look like delicate and otherworldly sculptures. At the start of *giđđadálvi*, the temperatures also warm considerably, making it possible to spend time outside in the sweet, fresh air, skiing, walking, ice fishing. Sometimes perihelions magically appear – atmospheric tricks of the eye, which make it look as if three suns, shaped like golden diamonds, are beating down on creation instead of just one. It is Easter time, and hope and the coming of spring can be felt in the glint of every snow crystal, carried on the warming breeze, and seen on the pleasantly sun-kissed faces of nearly everyone in the village.

Easter is the essential event of Kautokeino because of the Sámi Easter Festival and Easter week. In the olden days, Easter week was a time for weddings and baptisms and confirmations, before herders dispersed for summer pastures with their reindeer. Confirmations are central to Easter week and are a rite of passage for many Norwegian kids, and Kautokeino is no exception. Parents save for the event; it requires a massive outlay of cash, for new *gákti* and new silver pieces to go with the traditional dress, as well as private parties for family and friends celebrating the confirmed. Any person who has ever googled 'Sámi people' is likely to first see pictures of kids from Kautokeino dressed in their traditional finery on confirmation day, young and fresh faced in colourful new *gákti* that have taken months to sew by mothers or grandmothers or special *gákti* makers. After the church confirmation ceremony, of which there may be two or three depending on the number of kids being confirmed that year, confirmation classes gather on the steps of the Kautokeino Kirke, a long red church at the end of the village, triumphant from having made it through classes and being confirmed in the Church of Norway, a symbolic gesture of the turn into adulthood. Enter almost any Sámi home and you will find three sets of pictures on the walls: wedding, baptism and confirmation. Tourists often show up outside of the church to take pictures of the kids as they have their photos taken by family members, something that I find weird and unsettling, given that the children have just completed an important religious event and are complete strangers to the tourists, but it happens every year.

Holidays in Norway are always signalled by the arrival of particular products that are only seasonally sold in the stores; at Christmas, it's the Jul Brus, a holiday soda, and *pepperkaker*, or gingersnaps. At Easter time, and specifically in Kautokeino, it's the arrival of Vivi's mobile hjemmebakeri, a bakery from Alta filled with carrot cakes and doughnuts and all manner of sweets that sets up shop in the parking lot of the Statoil, the most highly trafficked spot in the village. Easter festivities go all week long in Kautokeino, from church services to open market stalls in which old women sell their *duodji* (handicrafts) and reindeer boots and antlers to the hundreds and hundreds of tourists that descend upon the town. Knowing that this is when most of the *áhkut* (grandmothers) will be out and about, a clever sewing-machine company sets up a mobile store in the centre of the village, out of a large freight truck. There are concerts at night, and because April in Norway is full of red days – days in which everything is closed, owning to Maundy Thursday, Good Friday and Easter – people are largely free of responsibility and ready to celebrate. With the weather stable at this time of year, even the reindeer herders generally have time off.

The week begins with an ice-fishing contest at Suohpatjávri, a lake just outside the village; everyone buys a ticket to participate and prizes are won for the biggest fish caught as well as the smallest. There is also a drawing for a car, which usually remains parked outside of the Rema 1000 for a week or two in advance, inspiring everyone to buy ticket over ticket in the hopes of winning. I am not inured to this tactic; having made it several months without any form of transportation, I dream of having a car and so buy a ticket just in case.

On the lake, a burly contest worker walks around with a giant red drill, making holes in the ice, and people sit for hours with their cups of coffee, camped out on reindeer skins, fishing poles dipped in the freezing water, hoping for a fleshy pink Arctic char to win them a cash prize or the lucky car. The men at the local hardware store try to teach me about proper bait for fishing, and I find myself with a refrigerator full of something called 'power maggots', electric pink creatures that look as if they were sourced in Chernobyl, and also some traditional non-glowing worms in soil, sold in Styrofoam cups. I laugh every time I look in the fridge to see what meaningful contents now constitute for me: power maggots and reindeer meat, a complete turnaround from the micro greens, cheese and kombucha that would have been in my fridge in New York.

I'm slowly becoming less self-conscious about joining activities in the village, and so I venture out for the ice-fishing contest and then the Sámi Grand Prix, an annual joiking contest for all of Sápmi, with participants from Sweden, Norway, Finland and Russia.

The joik is a powerful song form; it sounds like something otherworldly, with guttural thrusts and a sort of yodelling, sometimes with words and sometimes not. Without understanding its significance or history, it could be dismissed as random nonsense sounds, but joiks are an emotional expression of the deepest nature; they are spiritual acts and a joik can be made about a person or place or feeling. It is an ancient song form – possibly one of the oldest in Europe – that survived Christian missionaries and Norwegianization, which shunned anything that was not unilaterally mainstream Norwegian. Joiking was never officially outlawed, but was not destigmatized publicly until great Sámi musicians and artists such as

Nils-Aslak Valkeapää and Mari Boine started to bring it into the light, to wider audiences. Now the grand prix has become an annual showcase of joiking and its regional variances, and is an event of cultural pride as much as anything. The joik contest is coupled with an original song contest and is always held in the local sports hall, Báktehárji, and broadcast on TV on NRK Sápmi.

After the grand prix, there are always a couple of big parties and concerts at the local hotel and the Báktehárji that will go on until morning. In the Arctic, evening events don't really start until well after 11 p.m.; walk into Alfred's Kro, the local pub, any time before that and you will find an entirely empty space. I would like to go to these evening events, but I'm still too worried about running into Áilu, or that I will be alone with no one to talk to. Most of all, I worry that people will talk about me. Kautokeino is a small town, and I don't want anyone getting the impression that I am loose or untoward. I'm surprised about why this matters to me, but it has much to do with not wanting to stand out or call attention to myself. The previous fall, a French journalist based in Stockholm who covered the north for the newspaper *Le Monde* came to Kautokeino as research for a book he was writing. He was an acquaintance I'd made through a friend, and I invited him to dinner to meet Áilu. Earlier that day I'd spotted him in the village doing interviews and asked him for a ride home because I was carrying heavy groceries. When I got out of the car, he kissed me in the French way – a quick peck on each cheek that defines hellos and goodbyes. Within one hour Áilu had received messages from two separate people that I had been kissing another man in front of our house.

Rumours, gossip: they travel quickly here, and it just isn't worth the bother.

It is early in the morning on Easter Sunday when there is a knock on my door: it's Áilu, wearing his *gákti*, staggering, clearly drunk out of his mind as if he's been partying for the last several days. Eyes half-closed and trying to steady himself in the doorway, he asks to come in but I turn him away. It's difficult to unpack my feelings for him – anger for leaving in the way that he did and resentment for what I see as a humiliation – possibly the most useless and unproductive human feeling one can have, but present for me in abundance nonetheless. But mostly, I'd been scarred so deeply in the past, and abrupt abandonment – of which being left alone in the Arctic certainly qualified in my book – triggered such a visceral, painful set of feelings and need for self-protection that it shut me down completely. I considered that to be my greatest superpower, hard earned and nascent as it was – learning to find safety in myself in the face of upheaval.

In lieu of going out at night, on weekends I start to reconnect with people from home. I don't want to be back in America, but maintaining contact with some of my friends – or re-establishing connections – feels important, mostly because now I feel as if I'm starting to gain some clarity about the people who have been important to me in the past and people to whom I owe apologies for when everything was falling apart. I think about people when I see them on Facebook, like Molly, a woman who worked for me when I was struggling to keep my business going, overcome by stress and fear that I could not talk about out of my tremendous sense of shame. I'd had to lay Molly off, and I wasn't gracious about it in the process. I decide to make contact with her again, expressly to say I am so sorry for the times that I was awful to her: it was my fault. It feels good to be able to do this and, more importantly, to see there was a foundation of real friendship behind all that had happened.

I am also starting to recognize, in my aloneness and in self-reflection, how much my ego and need to be accepted by certain people – people who I thought were friends but are now nowhere to be found – and desire for their inclusion and acceptance had influenced my decision-making and led me to walk away from many people who were genuine friends. This shallowness wasn't intentional, but it was pervasive in the circles in which I had worked and lived. With a clarity that only the sting of rejection can bring, I see it for what it is now – a huge character deficit, and I could only become conscious of this emptiness when I was outside of New York, away from social media and giving a shit about what made a person important or relevant or 'worthy'. I think about one woman in particular, my friend Tracy, whom I see from time to time posting on Facebook. At one time we'd been close but lost contact; we'd worked together for an organization that was my client and where she was employed. Tracy was gorgeous, an event producer and the daughter of a pilot, which means that she was laser focused in getting things done and done properly. Tracy was unflappable; I once watched her organize an event for two hundred people in forty-eight hours on a shoestring budget, from finding a venue and planning all aspects down to arranging flowers for the bathrooms to make sure they were elegant enough. I'd travelled with Tracy to San Francisco and then on the long journey to Africa for work; she was an inveterate animal lover who owned two dogs, two pigeons, two doves and two cats in New York. I watched her hand-feed giant terrifying-looking buzzards outside of our hotel in Tanzania the day before she left to climb Mount Kilimanjaro. Tracy had gone on a Native American vision quest in Utah, surviving in the desert with a tarp and a water bottle. She dressed to the nines and could tell you the provenance of any high-end fashion item, but could be equally at ease hanging out with a bunch of locals in a honky-tonk bar. She wasn't afraid to speak truth to power; she did not like Richard and told me as much, and when the marriage went south, she was the first person to find me a shrink and lend me a shoulder to cry on. But we fell out of touch when she abruptly left the project we'd both worked on, and I was unclear on what had happened – I only understood from my client that I should not ask questions because it was none of my business. Time passed and we lost contact. And I missed Tracy.

I reach out to her and we reconnect on Skype. She's astonished to learn of my journey from New York to the Arctic, and it's as if no time has ever passed between us. She says 'what the fuck!' a lot, and I absolutely love talking to her, her no bullshit, plain-spoken manner and her openness. I ask why she'd left the project on which we'd both worked; she'd been a rising star, was generating money and was well liked by everyone she met. I am gobsmacked to learn, through several conversations, she was fired, a move orchestrated by the same person who'd given me so much grief. So much of her experience mirrored my own, and I feel surprised to learn that

I wasn't alone. I also feel great shame for not having known and not having stood up for her, something I wished someone had done for me.

*

Sámi language exams are approaching. I'm half-heartedly trying to study, and as I flip through the formal English to Sámi dictionary that I miraculously find, though it appears ancient, I'm conscious there is no way I'll pass the exams, and I might as well sit them out. I'm also pretty sure that words like *large intestine monocle, fallow deer* and *ruddy turnstone* are not ones I'll get much use out of in regular conversation. I give the school notice that I'm not going to take the tests, because I know I'll fail. My conversational skills are very basic but passable, and for now, it's the best that I can do.

Although we haven't seen each other for some time, I do keep in regular touch with Per, the former journalist and military veteran I'd met in London. Per lives in Oslo with his partner and young son, and we catch up every three months or so via Skype. I relish our conversations in particular because Per is the only person in my orbit who has first-hand knowledge of the two worlds I am straddling, and he is such a wise dispenser of advice that he really has, as I'd felt when I first met him, become like a wise brother figure to me.

I reveal to Per during one of our calls that I've broken up with Áilu and have been alone in Kautokeino.

On hearing this news, and without hesitation, he tells me that he's flying up the following weekend and do I have a place for him to stay. I let him know that I'm fine, and it's not necessary, but he's insistent. He arrives a week later, just as the sun is starting to make visible headway in melting the metres and metres of snow, searing it into cold liquid, causing great gushing melts of muddy water that flow with abandon everywhere, so prolific you can hear it glopping down streets and liquefying streams that now surge with glorious abandon. Only in the Arctic can the power of the sun and its impact on the seasons be felt in such a dramatic and particular way, so full of life and vigour.

Per arrives in a rental car from Alta and quietly checks out my accommodation. Ordinarily, I'd be worried about gossip, but I am alone now and it is clear from his rental car that Per is an out-of-town visitor who could be anyone. And besides, my desire to spend time with him eclipses any fear of tittle-tattle. I explain to him what happened over reindeer pizza at Pitstop, a local pizza place from which Bealjážat, two mountains that look like ears and are named as such, can be seen clearly in the distance, still snow-capped and dramatically set against a cloudless and deep blue sky. We sit outside. 'I had to come, Laura,' he says, looking over the mountains. 'I feel somewhat responsible for you arriving in this part of the world,' he explains, referring to his suggestion that I visit Norway in the first place and introducing me to Mikko. Of course, it's not his fault at all. This was a faultless situation; if anything, he opened the door to a new world.

Per is visibly taken aback when I exchange pleasantries with people in Sámi, and that instead of my usual New York attire I'm now wearing fleeces and multipocketed hunter's pants, living in the most basic of apartments with a giant hunting knife hanging in the kitchen. It's good to see Per, and to be around someone who understands my old life but also understands the life I've entered. 'You know that the north is nothing like the rest of Norway, don't you? This is a completely different universe.'

I show him around the village, and we talk late into the night before retiring. The next morning, he hears me admonishing next-door neighbour Nils, who is outside talking loudly, to be quiet. Per comes out and lights a cigarette, silent as he surveys the landscape and kicks up gravel with his boots. 'You know, Laura, it's difficult to tell if you are crazy, or brave, or both.'

13

BOO

If there is one thing that I carry with me as evidence of both nature and nurture, it is my love of cleaning, which is surely genetic as much as it is conditional. Cleaning reminds me of the past, and of Grammie, who joyfully taught me how to properly polish silver and who ironed her bed sheets into crisp attention and always made sure the carpets were vacuumed and bric-a-brac was dust-free and pristine. If you have things, you must keep them nice, I learned from her. Her house always smelled of Pledge furniture polish and warm spray starch, smells that conjure security for me. One of the greatest gifts Joan gave me was the insistence on keeping things neat; even when a maid came weekly, I was not allowed to have my room cleaned unless I'd had everything picked up off the floor, clothes hung, papers in drawers. I wasn't to go to school unless my bed was made and my room was presentable enough for an open door. It doesn't take a psychiatrist to know what I already know: I love cleaning because it gives me a sense of order and control; it is also the singular side benefit of having self-diagnosed OCD. I may have to check the house fifty times to make sure that I've turned off all the hob burners and unplugged the toaster, but my God, look at how all the spice jars are lined up so neatly! I love the tangible reordering of chaos into organized existence, all under my domain. The world may fall apart tomorrow but I am in control of spotless baseboards and visible dust.

I discover so many tips about cleaning in the Arctic that I'm often in a sort of bizarre janitorial nirvana. I learn that particularly cold, dry days in winter, when the snow is hard and grainy, are the ideal time to take your largest rugs outside, cover them in snow and vigorously beat them with a carpet beater or broom to freshen and cleanse them. I learn that in lieu of dry cleaning – something that doesn't exist *at all* in the Arctic and for which I can't find words, even in Norwegian – intricate *gákti* are cleaned by hanging them out in bitter cold, with a bit of snow if they are particularly dirty. I learn that Finnish Koskenkorva vodka (60 per cent alcohol!) will take away the scent of anything – pet stains, smoke, the most pungent body odour – by simply spraying it generously on the offending stain or fabric, miraculously also taking it the smell of vodka with it.

The apartment is threadbare and, as such, it becomes even more important to me to keep it clean and organized in order not to look entirely shoddy. And now it's spring, with the mountains of mud giving way to the earliest whispers of flora and fauna that will soon shoot up all around us. I can feel the energy in the air and it makes me want to spring clean, so one Saturday I set about degreasing the fat-splattered oven with baking soda paste, flipping the torn mattresses and cleaning the windows with vinegar. Cleaning products are limited in the north, with nowhere near the variety found in the US or the UK, so I use *grønn sope*, an all-purpose viscous soap the colour of tree sap that fills the apartment with the powerful scent of pine.

Boo and Rennie, the cats, have been content to spend the winter inside the apartment, cosy by the fire or tucked under the thick duvets on my bed. But now Boo in particular spends most of his time at the window, making peepy and insistent meows at the panoply of nature taking place in front of him, from flitting juvenile sparrows and giant bobbing black and white magpies, to a red fox that dashes by the window often, and even a giant Arctic hare that appears in the early mornings in advance of the fox. It must be the equivalent of binge-watching Netflix for cats, and I can only imagine what Boo is thinking as he sits there, a cat from Harlem who has never been outside, save for in a carrier, observing the world through his mesh bag on the long and arduous journey here in taxis, planes and trains, but never free to roam outside on his own.

As the days go by, it's as if a primal internal switch has suddenly been flipped, Boo paces the apartment furiously, his little body hot with agitation about every-thing he's seeing and smelling outside. Sometimes, in a fit of frustration, he will even jump on the lever-shaped door handles in an attempt to open the doors. He meows relentlessly. As much as I would like to let him out, I know this could spell disaster should he roam too far, and Rennie and Boo are like my children, precious to me, my closest companions here.

One day while cleaning, I open some high windows

in the kitchen; I need to get some fresh air into the apartment. The windows are only partially open, barely wide enough for a large mouse to enter. I go about my cleaning in the bedroom and bathroom and, after a bit, notice that I only see Rennie in the apartment. I check the kitchen window and see that it has been pushed open. Boo has escaped.

Frantic, I close all the windows and throw on my shoes and run outside calling for Boo – up and down our street, behind the apartment building, at the kindergarten across from where I live, and in the adjacent gully. He is nowhere. I tell myself that he will return in a few hours; cats always return if given enough time. I nervously wait. Day turns to dusk, and then night, and Boo is not to be found. I am beside myself. I remember reading somewhere that if you are missing a cat, or new to an area, you should put a piece of your clothing near the front door so the cat can pick up the scent and return home. I take a well-worn jumper out of the laundry and put it under my bedroom window, hoping it will catch on the wind and Boo will smell his way home to me, safe.

One day turns into two and then three, and there is still no sign of Boo. I need to spread the word in the local community that Boo is missing, a verb I do not know in Sámi. Inexplicably, and thankfully, Facebook is a central transom for news and information in our village, though most of the posts are in Sámi, a language unrecognized by the platform and thus untranslatable unless one speaks it. I find a picture of Boo sitting in a box on the day we moved out of my apartment in New York, and get help writing a Facebook post in Sámi and Norwegian. I make posters and copy them at the university – 'busa *le javkan!'* (missing cat). Bjarne lets me post one in the window at the petrol station, a sight that, in retrospect, I'm sure made many herders and truck drivers chuckle as they passed through for coffee and petrol. People don't treat animals in such a precious way in this part of the world, and Boo is a cat. A cat from New York.

A week passes, and then two. There isn't a day that I don't wake up fretting about Boo, where he is, what he's doing, if he's finding food. Did someone catch him? Was he taken by a fox? I google whether or not foxes eat cats and am relieved to learn that they don't. I walk up and down the streets and in the fields, calling for him and trying hard not to cry visibly. The loss of Boo is like a gut punch to my soul; I brought him all the way here and now he is in peril and there is nothing I can do to help him. I pray, a lot. When I'd first lived in Los Angeles with Kathleen, my Catholic Irish friend, I learned about the world of patron saints, and Kathleen's mother taught me that I should pray to St Anthony, the patron saint of the poor and small requests, whenever something went missing. I tried it a few times over the years – mostly with keys and small objects – and, miraculously, it always worked. And so now I had St Anthony on celestial speed dial, praying hard every day that he'd help Boo on his way home.

What had I done? Boo was my heart from the day that I'd picked him up in Harlem with his runny nose and unusually long body, coloured like a Belted Galloway cow in giant spots of black and white. Boo had been with me through everything in recent years, and I'd dragged him from the safe comfort of his home in New York all the way to the top of the earth, only for this to happen. It tortured me, because the only thing worse for someone who has experienced life-changing loss is to know that someone or something they love is experiencing that same pain. Abandoned animals, orphans – these were triggers for me that caused crippling stabs of anxiety and anguish, even if I didn't know the victims personally. Now, this was my cat. I imagine what it would feel like if this were an actual child, and I know with absolute certainty that I would not survive such loss and I spiral into thinking about all the people who have experienced such grief. My mind cannot stop going down the rabbit hole.

Slowly, because of my Facebook posts, people start to engage with me. Once or twice when I was with Áilu, a man named Mikko G, who lived in the nearby village of Mieron, would come by with friends. His brother was a herder who lived next door to our apartment. Now Mikko G messages me – he will help me look for the cat. He appears at the house silently and drives around with me day after day. He sits and has coffee with me, also mostly silently – something I love about Sámi culture is that words are not always needed to fill time and space: it is just about the presence of another person in that space with you, helping to avoid the aloneness.

The loss of Boo forces me to get out in the village and interact in ways that I normally wouldn't, posting flyers at the local market and hardware store and at the petrol station. Everyone now knows the story of Boo the New York City cat, lost in the wilds of the north, and people come forward all the time to ask me if I have found him or offer sightings, which never seem to pan out. Gerlinde, Bernt Morten's girlfriend whom I so wanted to know better, comes over to help me look for Boo and spends hours walking around the marshlands near my house and down by the river. Gerlinde calms me and starts to teach me about the nature around us as we walk and call for him. Still there is no Boo. A month has passed.

*

One day, I get a message on Facebook out of the blue from my friends Tiziano and Luca, two Italians from Rome whom I'd met nearly thirty years earlier, when I was living in Los Angeles. Mary, the flight attendant from Supercuts, had called me on the City desk at the *Times* one Saturday and asked me if I wanted to go to Europe for the first time because she couldn't use a ticket she had for a planned trip. 'It's $35 to Rome but you have to stay for three weeks and the ticket is for in three days,' she said. In an unconsidered fit of wanderlust, I took the ticket and ended up in Italy, pre-Internet, having picked a hotel, a *pensione* called the Palladium Palace, near the train station from a giant reference book I found at the Foreign desk at the newspaper.

I had never been in a foreign country before, and Italy was a particular experience for a young blonde woman travelling alone. From the moment I got off the plane, I was overwhelmed and terrified by the overzealous men clucking and ogling and approaching me as I tried to figure out where to go. No one spoke a lick of English, and I was petrified. When I finally made it to the hotel, I was further alarmed to see a shower with no shower stall, a sink and a simple cot in the room; I'd not understood the austere nature of a simple *pensione*. Terrified to leave, knowing I had three weeks in Italy, I stayed locked in my room drinking water from the bathroom tap and rereading the only book I'd brought, *The Color Purple*, over and over for three days until the hotel became worried about me and a kindly front-desk worker named Gianfranco left some food outside my door. From that act of kindness, I mustered the courage to venture out, making friends with Gianfranco and two other desk people, Ettore and Tiziano, and eventually Luca, whose father it turned out owned the hotel. We all became friends and they showed me around Rome, inviting me out with their friends and families. On my last day, Luca's father gave me a hug and erased half of my hotel bill, telling me that he had a daughter of my age and he always wanted me to remember my first trip to Italy.

I would return to Italy many times – Luca and Gianfranco visited me in California, and Tiziano and his wife took me out to dinner with Richard the night before we headed south to get married – but I hadn't talked to Luca and Tiziano for years. Now Tiziano is reaching out to let me know that he and Luca have been on a wilderness trip to Svalbard, the Norwegian archipelago between mainland Europe and the North Pole in the Arctic Ocean. They want to come to mainland Norway and visit me in Kautokeino. They've also been following the saga of Boo the cat on social media and want to help me find him.

I am astonished.

I rent a car and pick Tiziano and Luca up in Alta, the single-lane road to Kautokeino gloriously choked with reindeer languidly grazing on lichen in the newly melted snow making an unforgettable welcome for them both.

It is as if no time has passed between us, as we drive and chat and catch up on our lives, which includes marriages, divorce, graduation and kids. After Tiziano and Luca drop off their things, we walk through Kautokeino calling for Boo, and we stop in a large marshy area bordered by the Sámi museum, Maritex, a Sámi dry goods store where bolts of *gákti* cloth and ribbons are sold, and Kautokeino Sølvsmie, a goldsmith's shop. In Maritex, the woman at the counter tells me she thinks she's seen Boo in the area, but I am not overwhelmed by the news; many people have believed they've spotted Boo in various places, but to no avail. Just in case, we go into the goldsmith's to ask, and Luca seems to pause when he hears Franz Singer, the proprietor, speak. As it turns out, Franz is Italian, from the north of Italy, married to a Sámi woman. Here, in Kautokeino – an Italian! Luca and Tizano excitedly talk to him in their lilting mother tongue, gesticulating wildly and explaining the missing cat and to please be on the lookout.

I should not be so surprised by Franz's presence; it makes sense, in that Kautokeino, as much as it is a reindeer-herding village, is also a little-known home to artisans. It started in the 1950s, with an adventurous and exceedingly self-reliant Danish man called Frank Juhls.

Frank came to Kautokeino when there were no roads leading to the village and very few outsiders. Kautokeino was remote and secluded, even to many Norwegians. From scratch, Frank built a cabin and a studio high on a ridge overlooking the village, adding to it year after year, making his living by repairing Sámi jewellery, which is central to traditional Sámi dress, from shiny silver brooches worn by women called *risku* to the buttons and tips that adorn belts, the former of which are central to identifying if someone is married or single. Finding an underserved market, the business grew exponentially. As a nomadic culture, the Sámi had historically used silver as an important form of savings – it was easily portable and could be traded or sold in hard times. Silver jewellery was never made by the Sámi, but obtained, and Frank was talented and easily found a market creating Sámi jewellery, along with his German wife, Regine, a gifted artist in her own right, and eventually they also started making their own modern designs. As Frank's business grew, so too did the need for master craftspeople, and traditionally trained goldsmiths started to come to work at Juhls', making Sámi jewellery and, in their off time, working on their own designs, living in tidy cabins adjacent to the workshop, in solitary lives inspired by nature. Most of the foreigners who settled in Kautokeino or stayed for any period of time, save for a doctor or teacher or two, were usually goldsmiths (the correct name for people who create out of metal, no matter the type) because this was one of the few places in the world where traditional artisans could practise their detailed craft and make a reasonable and consistent living at the same time. Gerlinde had started at Juhls', and so had an older, kindly Swiss couple near the marsh named Peter and Anita, who now had their own shop. The Juhls' gallery itself had grown into something magical and incongruous to the surrounding village over the years: inside the giant main building, shaped like a pagoda, could be found a shop filled with unexpected and numerous treasures, a room filled with thick Middle Eastern carpets, a room with a black grand piano and a wall of Frank's modernist artwork and highly curated bric-a-brac from all over Scandinavia, an observatory for the Juhls' egg-laying hens, and a room with traditional Sámi *duodji*, as well as the shop's primary *raison d'être*, silver for sale, everywhere. There was a giant golden thumb made of mosaic on which the elderly Frank was constantly working, as well as a mosaic wall that Regine worked on regularly for years on end, each day a little more progress made. Juhls' was an epicentre of creativity, bringing a touch of international feeling to Kautokeino.

We search for Boo, but to no avail, and Luca and Tiziano decide that they want to make me a traditional Italian dinner. Unimpressed by what's available in the local grocery store, and with a certain amount of freedom because of the rental car, we make the drive across the Finnish border thirty minutes away to a small grocery store in a village called Hætta. Finland is on the euro, and therefore much cheaper for petrol and almost everything else, so many people cross the border for a monthly grocery shop or to fill up on petrol or alcohol, careful to stay within the limits of how much can be brought back. I rarely go to Heatta because I don't have a car, and, frankly, there is something about the village that slightly depresses me. But Luca and Tiziano scour the aisles of the store, coming out with bottles of wine and olive oil and limp basil and major-brand spaghetti. They come back to my apartment and cook all afternoon, creating an absolute feast that goes on course after course. In the morning, they depart for home, and I'm struck with a profound sadness at being alone again.

*

The days are filled with a steady, cold, constant rain that leaves me distraught about Boo and how he can possibly be surviving. I can't bring myself to think of him dead, but with each day my hope fades a bit. I talk to Tracy often – she has some experience with lost pets, notably her own beloved cat, which she called Clam, who was never found. One day Tracy suggests that I should call a man in America called Tim Link, who is known as an animal communicator. He specializes in locating missing pets remotely, and I check his website to find glowing testimonials for cats and dogs from all over the United States that he has found by connecting with them mentally. It sounds crazy, but I've seen enough in my life, and in the north, to know that there *are* people who can connect with other species and realms, and find lost objects and predict the future. I've tried everything else, and I'm desperate to find Boo, and so I send Tim an email and he responds immediately, asking for a picture of Boo and my general location. He tells me that he'll make contact with Boo. I hear from him a short while later: he says that Boo is alive, and then gives me extremely detailed information about his condition, that he's been staying outside but found shelter, and references numerous small landmarks that could not be known through Google Maps or any other means explainable by a sceptic. He tells me that Boo has shown him motors running around him and describes ATVs, which of course belong to the reindeer herders getting ready to depart for the summer. He also gives me a map of 'hotspots' where he believes Boo is roaming, and tells me not to walk and call his name, as trying to follow a moving voice is confusing to lost animals. He tells me that he's let Boo know that I am looking for him.

Kautokeino in summer is largely devoid of people, who have now gone to their summer pastures at the coast or to their cabins in Sweden and elsewhere. The village is quiet, with miles and miles and miles of open tundra just beyond, low and lush silver birch, gigantic patches of purple and green fireweed, and a sun so bright and powerful that it illuminates everything with an all-encompassing glow. It's as if you can feel the earth eating up all its energy and using it to manifest this verdant landscape that will only exist for a few months before falling dormant again. The sun has moved to being out twenty-four hours now, leading to the necessity of purchasing a large blackout curtain for the bedroom window. It is difficult to sleep, nonetheless; although you can make a room dark, the act of falling asleep, I become convinced, is largely contingent on fading light to signal a winding down for the brain.

The few children and families that do remain in the village are up at all hours, with kids out riding bikes and jumping on trampolines. This is a safe place and, with no darkness, in many ways, time ceases to exist. The mosquitos come out en masse; Kautokeino is the European capital of mosquitos, and I have to hang nets over the windows and burn citronella candles to keep them out. As annoying as non-malarial mosquitos may be, they serve an important function in that they feed the thousands of birds that stop in the north for the summer, and also drive reindeer to lower elevations, where costal breezes keep the mosquitos from being as much of a nuisance.

Stine has been south with her kids to visit her father in Fredrikstad. She is tiring of Kautokeino and starts to make rumblings about moving. 'It's difficult here and I want my kids to see something bigger, and to have more possibility,' she tells me. I know it is tough for her, raising the kids alone, with no support in their care, frustrated also by not being brought fully into the fold of her in-laws' family, even though her kids are half-Sámi. She is accepted marginally but not embraced. The trip to the south that strengthens her resolve to leave, and I fear that she'll be gone before fall, in order to get kids situated in school. She begins to talk about selling her house and my heart hurts just thinking about her leaving.

One morning at two or three, I see my upstairs neighbour in the mist, walking home from a visit to a friend, tiptoeing through the fireweed. Recently, an adorable puppy has often been tethered outside at the side of her apartment, visible from my kitchen window, but I haven't gone to say hello or give him a pet because I know that people can be tetchy about their animals here. As I'm looking out my window, she waves, giving me a warm smile before going inside. This is the first time I've seen her up close. The next afternoon, she appears at my door with a bowl of fresh summer fruit and cream. Her name is Tildá, and she's also been waiting for the right time to come and introduce herself. She is a sea Sámi, from the coastal village of Bodø, living with two of her kids in the apartment above. The dog is named Guvge. 'I know you have been alone and missing your cat,' she tells me in perfect English. As it turns out, Tildá rescues cats often and promises to keep an eye out for Boo. 'Don't worry, dear Laura, your Boo will return!'

I want so much to believe her, but every day my hope fades, and I am unable to cope with the idea of his loss, a thought too difficult to bear.

14

THE OTHERS

With most of the village gone for the summer, it feels as if I have the Arctic to myself. The sun in its twenty-four-hour brilliance makes it impossible to sit still, and I spend hours walking out on the tundra, the loamy earth spongy under my feet, literally putting a spring in each step. The land is so vibrant with growth and bloom and birth that you can almost feel it hum. My favourite hike passes unceremoniously by the local dump, oddly situated a few kilometres outside of the village adjacent to a large and gorgeous lake. The path is called Ginalvárri, and takes one higher and higher on the *vidda*, through the low silver pines and scrub, up until reaching an open expanse in which the sun seems to brush the earth and the clouds can nearly be touched they hang so low, a sight at which I constantly marvel. The sun is brutal and strong, making it possible to be sunburned within minutes. The top of Ginalvárri is marked by a bench and a metal box containing notebook and a pen for visitors to sign their names; it is one of the primary routes for hikers. I like to walk Ginalvárri early in the morning, with a hot Thermos of coffee and some dried reindeer meat, alone with my thoughts. Occasionally a plane will fly by high overhead, bound for India and the Gulf States, something I learned by looking at online flight trackers. I wonder if the people high above can see me, a tiny fleck beneath the clouds, lost in nature like a flea in the hair of a dog.

Money is tight. Very, very tight. Because there is very little to buy here, and very little money to spend, I see my shopping habits changing profoundly according to my new definition of 'need'. I'm learning how to eat off the land from Gerlinde – things like how to use dandelion leaves in salad and to make tea out of fireweed leaves. I buy very little at the grocery store – flour, butter, oil, salt and coffee, mostly. I start to make my own breads and cook potatoes in every conceivable way: boiled, baked, fried and mashed. Sometimes I go fishing with a very quiet young Danish man named Benjamin, a goldsmith who works at Juhls'. Benjamin is gentle and reserved. He has an old white Nissan and he comes to my place on Ájagohpi to pick me up. From there we drive to the southern end of the village and leave the car, hiking in silence, bushwhacking through the deep reeds, until we settle on a lake, where Benjamin patiently teaches me how to fish there, from baiting the hook to casting a line. The fish are so plentiful in these pristine Arctic lakes that it is almost impossible to come up empty handed. When I was in Sámi language school, we once went on a fishing trip to learn the names of fish and fishing-related activities in Sámi. A couple of students went out on a boat with a wide green fishing net, and I was astonished to see them return with dozens of fish, as if some divine miracle of biblical proportions had transpired before our very eyes. Benjamin teaches me how to fillet the fish, and we always make a fire and sit cooking and eating our catch and drinking black coffee, swatting a multitude of mosquitos away from us. We each freeze the rest of the fish, which will become a winter staple for thick and hearty soups.

Stein gives me reporting jobs and this proves to be not only a financial lifeline, but also a way for me to start to learn more about the area in which I live. He sends me to Beaivváš Sámi Našunálateáhter, the Sámi theatre, to write about local productions, which are usually kids' shows in the summer and therefore easier to understand. Because I've been following American Sámi groups on Facebook, I start to write stories about the Sámi diaspora in the United States, from a man in Minnesota who started making traditional *lávvu* tents to elections for various Sámi American cultural groups and clubs.

But Stein also has me on the ready as his informal Kautokeino connection when breaking news requires it. Once, in one of the most this-person-could-not-be-less-qualified assignments, Stein tells me that he's heard about a raised terrorism alert along the northern border and asks me to go to our local police department and ask about any potential activity. To put this in context, the police department is one room across from the university, so small at the time that photos and processing for visas had to be done two hours away in Alta. 'Stein, I'm really not sure that I'm going to get any good information from the *politet*,' I tell him. 'I'm American, my Norwegian is almost non-existent and I don't know how to say "terrorist activity" in Sámi.'

'Go anyway,' he says.

I walk to the police department and ask in Sámi if I may speak English then ask matter-of-factly if there is any terrorist activity in the southern border with Finland. I believe that the officer wants to giggle – I'm sure of it. But she is straight faced. She shakes her head. 'I cannot tell you anything.'

Stein had a plan. I see it only in retrospect: the extent of his quiet and generous guidance in my life, helping to forge a path here when, really, there was no one else who could. In addition to giving me work to keep me going financially, he was doing something equally, if not more, important: he was sending me on these assignments to give me a place in the village, to help people contextualize me now that I was no longer the partner of a reindeer herder. It was also Stein's quiet and wise way of making me get out and engage with people when I felt very much like keeping to myself and becoming hermit-like. Stein was connecting me to my new world and making me learn about it on my own terms, a sort of forced exploration. And he was still – on top of mountains of his own work at the Karasjok bureau of *Ságat* – translating every single story of mine from English to Norwegian.

I need to start to think about my life in the north with more of a plan in place. I do not want to return to America; each day I feel as if I'm peeling off the layers of two onions. One is me, and who I really am in the absence of trying to be someone else – a person that I think others want me to be – in order to be loved and accepted.

The other is this place itself, this deeply, deeply unknowable place in which every day I am forced to stretch and learn and discover something new because there simply is no other choice. And the land, for some inexplicable reason, has for me a magnetic draw for which words are difficult. It is being in a space that leaves no choice but for self-reflection and meditation, cradled by nature all around me. Strangely, I am more alone than I've ever been, but I feel safe here. Nature is my endlessly fascinating companion, leaving me every day in awe of its complexity and power and the absolute interconnectedness of everything; of how nature works like the finest and most intricate machine ever created, where everything has a purpose and a divine symbiosis. I start to see it in small ways, from *luomi* – the Sámi name for the bright orange cloudberries that grow in late summer and have exceeding amounts of vitamin C to keep all who eat them going for the winter when the sun will not show itself – to the natural migration of the reindeer to the coast to escape the mosquitos and fatten up on the rich lichen that grows there in abundance. Nature has a plan, and I am learning every day with reverence.

Each day, I walk various paths in hope of spotting Boo. I miss him terribly and without pause. My guilt for losing him overpowers me with sharp anxiety attacks, and I often cry myself to sleep with worry about his whereabouts or condition. Regardless of whether or not it's rational, Boo's loss hits me at my core because it strikes at the heart of my most significant and deeply felt scars, scars that I like to keep hidden so that I can remain invulnerable to hurt. Boo being missing is a triggering reminder of abandonment, from the loss of my mother and Anna to the rejection of a mother who not only didn't want me, but also reviled me. I did not want to be the abandoner or the abandoned.

The woman at the dry goods store tells me she's sure she's seen Boo nearby on occasion; but minutes later in the village centre, a group of old Sámi reindeer herders who are gathered around the local bulletin board cluck at the missing poster of Boo and tell me in Sámi they are sure he's been taken by a hawk, given that he's black and white and looks like a moving target. Gerlinde thinks she's seen him once in her yard, trying to catch birds at dawn. People want to be helpful, but every day my hope diminishes. Boo has been gone two months to the day.

While Stein is giving me articles to write, I know that this is not a sustainable long-term career path and I need to have a larger plan in place if I am to stay here – not only for financial reasons. I had continued in class without sitting the exams, sure I would fail, but now, with school ending, I will need a visa to stay. An English teaching position is available at the local high school, which I refer to as 'reindeer-herding high' because it is where the reindeer herders go. My Sámi remains rudimentary, at best, but the one thing I have mastered to some degree is understanding the grammar and structural differences between English and Sámi and how to explain those differences, from conjugations to tenses. The other skill I have is knowing the words in Sámi related to reindeer herding, and I can translate them to English. I simplify my résumé, removing 'part of a Pulitzer team for the LA riots' and the other things that might be important anywhere else but seem meaningless in the context of this job, which is basically everything.

I really want this job and believe I'd be good at it, so I send my résumé to the school and I'm pleased and excited to be called in one day for an interview with the school rector, Ellen Inga Hætta, a traditional Sámi woman in her early sixties who is the beating heart of the school and a prominent member of the community. 'Takes guff from no one' is the phrase that first comes to mind with Ellen Inga; she has a direct stare and a commanding presence, even though she is soft and round and grandmotherly-looking at the same time.

The Samisk *videregående skole og reindriftsskole* was started to educate Sámi kids within their native culture, which means, in addition to studying the standard school subjects available everywhere, the students spend time learning advanced Sámi language skills, grammar, history, *duodji* and reindeer herding, the latter so important that reindeer herders even have a special academic schedule to fit their long stretches away helping their families with the herds. The school is part of the wider Norwegian efforts at language revitalization in that nearly all the classes are in Sámi. Ellen Inga speaks no English, or at least chooses not to, which I suspect for her is a matter of principle. I'm called in for my meeting and am led to a room to be interviewed by a panel that consists of Ellen Inga and two of the gym teachers, Jan Olav and Isak Ole. Ellen Inga, like many women of her age, is dressed in her *gákti*. I speak in shaky and elementary Sámi and can't remember ever being as nervous. Everyone is friendly and warm, but I am not called back for the job.

I learn that the university is starting a new programme in the autumn, a master's degree in indigenous journalism. I have no intention of being a journalist again as a career – finding that world much changed from my early days at the *Los Angeles Times* – but I see the programme, which will be taught in English and focus on indigenous considerations in journalism, as a way to learn more about the part of the world I inhabit, and I believe it could enhance my skills in media consulting. So I put in an application and wait to see what will happen. In addition to assignments for Stein, I have a few small consulting projects to keep me afloat in the meantime, and for now I am holding steady.

*

One Friday evening I'm home and engaged in the deeply exciting task of cleaning cabinets when Mikko G shows up unexpectedly with a few of his friends from Mieron, toting with them dozens and dozens of cans of Finnish beer. I notice immediately that Mikko G has an entirely new set of perfect white teeth that have replaced the old ones, which had become rotted stubs covered with nicotine. Mikko G was good-looking even with bad teeth, but now he looks like a minor TV celebrity. I trust Mikko G – he's been a solid friend. He has helped with Boo and driven me to Finland many times to buy cheap groceries. I like his company and know he's a good person, so I invite him in with the others to visit and share beers; as mostly everyone from the village is gone, I'm not worried about mushrooming gossip as I ordinarily would be. I know all three of Mikko G's friends casually: one is the son of the handyman who works for the local apartments, including mine, and another is an old friend of Áilu's who teaches herders at the high school and has been to visit the apartment before. His name is Samuel, and he is often crass and inappropriate, but somehow still likeable. His favourite line with me is 'Hey, Yankee, let's speak English', something that he repeats louder and more frequently as the night goes on. There is also a neighbour of Mikko G's named Per Ole, a slight man who is shy and introverted and gives the impression that he cannot believe that he's been invited to hang out in a woman's house. They are all bachelors, a very specific group of unmarried men in this part of the north who are in their thirties and forties or older and still live at home with their mothers.

The guys have been dropped off at my apartment; for this reason, it would have been difficult to turn them away even if I'd wanted to politely do so. In Norway, driving with almost any alcohol at all in one's system is a serious offence; culturally, here, it's seared into everyone's brains, even when completely inebriated, to just not drink and drive at all. People plan their drinking for this reason, and one of the most unexpected small businesses in Kautokeino is a taxi service of a few sedans that will drive drunken revellers from place to place at the weekend – it's that or have a designated driver willing to act as chauffeur for the evening. As reckless (or drunk) as I've ever seen anyone in Kautokeino – or in any village in the north, for that matter – I've never seen anyone irresponsible enough to drink drive, even if it's half a kilometre between houses on the same street when no one is around. It just isn't done.

We play music late into the night – a night that cannot be seen because the sun is fully up, and time becomes lost without the punctuation of sunrise and sunset. At one point I find myself dancing furiously in the living room to Bruce Springsteen with all of them at 3 a.m. It's later than

I can remember going to bed for ages, and I retire a short while later, pulling out mattresses and sheets and duvets before going to my room, waking up the next morning to a living room of grown men, passed out and snoring heavily. I make eggs and hash browns and coffee in the morning and everyone eats silently and departs. I'm not interested romantically in any of the people who have visited, but the evening, and the laughter, illuminates how deeply lonely I am, and I start to wonder if I could ever meet someone here who would understand me and with whom I could have a relationship. It's not that I pine for one; at this moment, my life is full with the challenge of simply getting by, but I often think about how nice it would be not to be alone, having to weather every experience on my own.

I'm also starting to surmise, from Áilu's perspective, what may have happened between us. At first it may have been interesting and novel to have a foreign girlfriend from New York, an urbanite from a culture so different, but at the end of the day, it must have been hard work, having to speak English, having to teach me customs and ways of being that were second nature to him. I must have been like a tether, a weight, and it was all too much. When I look at it this way, I even feel empathy for him and a sense of understanding. I know he's taken a bit of a beating in the village gossip mill for having left so abruptly. I learn through the same gossip mill that Áilu has a new girlfriend now; she's Sámi. Čáhppe still comes by the house frequently; he sits outside my window as if he's guarding me or checking in to make sure that I'm OK.

Tildá appears at my house for a visit two days after my late-night dance party. She's largely silent, as if searching for words; there's something she wants to say to me. I think she's going to caution me against male visitors or music that is too loud. She sits and smokes and, brow furrowed, after a coffee, it comes. 'Laura, you must not tell people that help you "I love you". Every man will think that you want to put your sock feet in the air for them.' It took a few minutes for me to grasp what she was talking about, but then it hit me: she was referring to something I'd reflexively exclaimed at the petrol station when someone offered to rent me a car for a day and I was exceedingly excited and grateful. Here, people do not say things they don't mean, and people certainly don't go around saying 'I love you' to acquaintances. Some people may only say that once a decade to their partners. I can't help but burst out laughing – not only at my own stupidity but also Tildá's honest concern and choice of words. She also bursts into hysterics, delighted that I understood what she meant. She was one single woman talking to another. But she's right; I know that the rules of engagement are different here, and I should probably shelve this casual expression of gratitude anyway. I'm not a valley girl, I'm not in California, and I'm well into my forties. Before Tildá leaves, there is one more thing. 'The men up here, they want to fuck and drink beers. So don't fuck them, and don't drink beers with them. Then you're special.' We break into hysterics again.

*

When you're alone most of the time, your observation becomes keen. When I walk outside or go to the store, I start to see all the people here that are not Sámi, and I wonder about their stories. I notice them now because I am one of them. When I first arrived, I was flummoxed that two small grocery stores filled with Norwegian food would have an entire aisle dedicated to Thai and Filipino food, until I learned that this is a significant minority culture in the north – women who married Sámi men and relocated to Kautokeino and other northern villages. The idea fascinates me. When I think about it as a New Yorker transplanted to the Arctic, with all the steep learning curves in my existence, I marvel at what these women have likely endured in leaving home for a place where literally everything is opposite – tropical temperatures, Buddhism and Hinduism, an abundance of cheap and copious fresh fruit and veg at the market, traded for minus-forty winters and dark nights, Christianity, a wildly different language and alphabet, mountains of snow and a culture and environment so different in almost every way. From the stories I hear in the village, the men usually meet these women on vacation; often, but not always, the men are considerably older. I see the women in the market, picking up food, sometimes with a child or two in tow. The couples marry and then sometimes relatives follow. Many kids in the village are half-Filipino and half-Sámi; there are two kids who are half-Sámi and half-African, and two kids who are half-Turkish and half-Sámi.

There are really many outsiders in the village: the goldsmiths from Juhls'; the foreign women who partner with Sámi men, like Gerlinde and Marit and Stine, who are Norwegian but foreign in that they are not Sámi. There is even a woman from Madagascar who married a Sámi man, and they have a grown son. The Norwegian teacher at the high school is Romanian, and one of the

English teachers is Irish. I think about these people more and more, and why we all chose this place, or why we choose to stay.

I recognize that we are united by our otherness and something else: we stay to face ourselves, to prove that we are strong, that we can survive through entirely dark winters of minus-forty-degrees temperatures that freeze your breath to ice but also make you remember that you have breath in you at all. And we stay because of a wild and untouched nature that overpowers and stuns and can make you cry: low white clouds gliding over teapot-blue skies, almost brushing the earth on a curve that you can follow with your hand; auroras that undulate and dance in electric greens and pinks and blues against a vanta black sky, never the same, never predictable, a gift that arrives unexpectedly in moments as mundane as taking out the garbage cans on a Monday night; the loamy tundra under your feet. This place makes a home for a particular kind of person, and for this reason, we are all kindred spirits in a way. We are alone together.

15

GRACE

There is a Sámi saying *ii leat jahki jagi viellja* – one year is not the brother of another year; the same could be said of one day and another. Everything changes.

I talk to Tracy nearly every week and, wisely, she tells me that I need to reconcile myself to the idea that Boo isn't coming back, that he had an incredible life filled with adventure and was living out his own destiny. The messages asking about Boo on Facebook from friends in all corners of the world for the three months that he's been gone are well meaning but making me terribly sad, and I know I need to come to terms with the hard and likely reality that Boo is gone, perhaps forever. The fireweed is slowly turning red and yellow and giving off its white down seedlings to the wind, the surest sign of the coming of autumn, along with rapidly dropping temperatures and a sun that is becoming gauzy as it starts slowly tucking in for the night. I can feel nature going into dormancy for the long winter to come. It is not a winter that Boo would likely survive if he's still alive.

I hold Rennie close and I say a prayer for Boo for the both of us, letting him go and wishing him well and that he is at peace. This may be one of the hardest types of losses of a pet, not being sure of their ultimate fate.

Others are going, too. Stine has decided that she is taking the kids and leaving Kautokeino because the aloneness is too much, and she wants her kids to be closer to where she comes from, nearer her father and dance lessons for the children and big shops and city life. She's been a dear friend to me, as well as a kindred spirit, and we spend one last night hanging out at her house, talking and laughing, listening to Motörhead, a band she loves, sharing some wine. She's going to sell her place, go south and complete her master's in education. I do not ask about her relationship; as much as I've come to know her, it feels inappropriate. The girls make a goodbye crayon drawing for me in which I'm a mermaid, which Stine gives me before I go home for the evening. I frame it and hang it in my kitchen so that I can look at it every day. Stine is gone within the week.

Happiness now comes from simple pleasures, and mine comes via fire. I've learned the secret to getting good firewood from a local seller and am delighted when a forklift comes with a gigantic bag filled with a whole cord of wood, delivered in front of my apartment. It is more wood than I've ever seen in one place, and it is hard and dry, which means it will burn well and is going to make the apartment deliciously warm and cosy. It was better than getting a Prada dress or a pair of Manolo Blahniks, or anything I could imagine that may have brought me delight in the past. I could not wait for it to get cold enough for my first fire, to smell the wood and the ash and the cold cast iron of the log burner getting hot for the first time.

Thoughts of all that I need to do to prepare for winter fill my head, and I'm at the kitchen sink rinsing potatoes one afternoon when Gerlinde bursts into my apartment, breathless and nearly screaming in her German accent. 'Laura! You must come now! I have seen Boo! I have really seen him! Come! Now!' We jump in her car and head to the giant marsh near the dry goods store and the Sámi museum, tall grasses everywhere. 'I was walking the path and I saw him but he ran away. He is really here!' We walk and call his name, but to no avail. There is no Boo. Earlier, Gerlinde had told her friends, the Swiss goldsmiths Peter and Anita, to keep an eye out for Boo because their shop sits at one side of the giant marsh. After nearly an hour of searching we give up and get in the car to go. When we are driving, the phone rings, and Gerlinde's eyes grow big. 'Peter and Anita have Boo! He is in the shop!'

We do a U-turn and speed to the shop, which Peter and Anita have temporarily closed to customers because of the visitor inside. We open the door, and there is Boo. Absolutely skeletal and dirty. He looks at me, and I look at him, and Boo jumps straight into my arms, meowing, purring, head butting and holding on to me for dear life. It is an absolute miracle on the tundra. A miracle. Boo had likely heard my voice and ran out of the marshes, where he might have been hidden for most of the summer.

I bring Boo home and call the vet, who advises me not to feed him too much or too quickly. I give him a can of food and he absolutely inhales it and then drinks an entire bowl of water. Rennie hisses at him and walks away, a reaction that I can only surmise is his expression of anger at Boo leaving him alone for so long. After eating and drinking, Boo curls up on the sofa and sleeps for three days straight. I imagine this is the first time that he's had any sort of feeling of safety or calm since he got lost. It feels like Christmas and winning the lottery and every other good surprise that a person could have coming at me at once. I think the gratitude may explode my heart.

Boo has become a minor celebrity; my world of social media buzzes with excitement over Boo the New York City wonder cat who survived the tundra and came back. Everyone in the village is talking about him, too. A friend who works in entertainment suggests that his story would be a great film, and others want me to write a children's book about Boo's adventures. For now, I don't want any of that. I'm just deeply grateful to have Boo, my miracle, back with us.

Without much fanfare, I hear from the university, and I've been accepted into the master's programme, but because of issues with visas for some of the other foreign students, the start of the programme will be delayed by several months, leaving me with unexpected time on my hands. I resume work on a feature magazine piece that I'd started ages ago about my move to the Arctic, but dropped when Áilu left and I'd had to focus on the prac-ticalities of daily life.

While I'm in the village, picking up groceries, I run into Bradan, the English teacher at the high school. Bradan is in his sixties, from Ireland and travels everywhere with a black and white sheep dog named Jimmy; they are an inseparable pair. Bradan has been in the village for years and he's the only other person I know in Kautokeino who doesn't have a car, so we often pass each other on foot while walking here or there and exchange brief pleasantries. I do not know Bradan well at all, but today he stops me with a look of seriousness in his eyes. 'Say, Laura, I'm not going to be teaching any more, and I told the school you'd be good as a teacher, given that English is your mother tongue and all,' he says in his sing-song Irish lilt. It is autumn now, halfway through the term, and an unusual time for new teachers to be hired. I wonder why he's giving up teaching, but don't pry. I also don't share that I'd interviewed for an English teaching position previously but the school never called back, and so I don't put much thought into it.

A week later, I get a call from Ellen Inga, on a Friday. She asks me in Sámi if I will come to the school on Saturday for a meeting. I can't refuse her – it would be rude – and so I take the appointment. She is with the other English teacher, who I deduce was hired instead of me when I'd applied earlier. He is a young Danish man in his early thirties called Viggo. He looks exactly like Shaggy from the cartoon *Scooby Doo*, so much so that his nickname is in fact Shaggy. In Ellen Inga's office, she's laid out waffles and strawberry jam and cream from a set of Tupperware containers. Viggo takes over most of the conversation in English. Bradan will no longer be teaching – reasons that can't be explained fully – but they are in desperate need of a second English teacher to take over his load, which will consist of teaching English to the reindeer herders, the *duodji* students and the kids who are studying auto mechanics and shop – technical studies. I present all the barriers to hiring me, telling Ellen Inga that I do consulting work so it may be necessary for me to travel at times, and I'm not sure about the teaching job any longer because of my changing schedule. 'We will work around you. We really need a teacher. Please, we really need a teacher.'

It doesn't take me long to say yes, for a few reasons, the most surface and practical of which are it will bring in some much needed additional income and fill time before the master's programme starts. But more importantly, it would connect me further to others here, helping me to create more of a sense of community. On my own here, as a single woman with no kids, it is virtually impossible to meet people in the ways others might – at the kindergarten among other parents or working in the fence with the reindeer. I am certainly not going to hang out at the bar at night in the hope of meeting people, because most of the people I'd want to know don't do that. Sure, I am becoming closer friends with Tildá upstairs, and I sit and drink coffee with her and chat, and also with Bjarne from the petrol station, who is a friend of Tildá's and often visits at the same time. I also spend time with Gerlinde, but she has a partner and a very busy life with her job as a costumer for the theatre and various film productions. This would give me a new way to meet friends, by way of colleagues, and to learn more about the reindeer-herding families and their kids.

There is also something bigger. I think I could be of service. Since I've arrived, I've struggled with the growing knowledge that much of the world is wholly unaware of the existence of Sámi people, and the culture is increasingly bombarded with a number of existential threats that go unnoticed internationally. Many times issues facing the Sámi remain in a silo – because while newspapers and radio discuss issues in the majority languages of Sápmi, Norwegian, Swedish, Finnish and Russian, very infrequently are these issues shared to a wider audience, in English, and further, by the people facing the issues themselves. Violations with respect to land rights, mining, wind farms, railroads, these are constant discussions in the north, but rarely are they covered in any great detail in English or with the benefit of historical knowledge or cultural context. If these kids could share more about their culture and perspectives and challenges in the lingua franca of the world, English, they may have more agency over their futures and a better chance at holding the megaphone on a global stage. I believe I have a mission to fulfil, and I suppose this is how it happens with all teachers who are enthusiastic about their work.

*

I share an office with Viggo in a separate building from the main part of the school. Bradan has gone to work in the library, and I slowly learn what's happened: he's simply burnt out from teaching but close to retirement, and so rather than have him quit, Ellen Inga has generously allowed him to switch jobs. Viggo is in his first year of teaching and is fresh and enthusiastic. He is currently living in the school, because of the Kautokeino housing shortage, in an area set-aside for school visitors, until other arrangements can be found.

Bradan's former desk is still covered with books and papers and exams and a dusty desktop computer. Viggo shares the teaching schedule with me, which will change nearly every week because of the reindeer herders' schedule; they are often out on the *vidda* with the reindeer, and everything revolves around nature first. Viggo will co-teach the herders' classes with me, at least to start. He shows me the textbooks and the next lesson, which inexplicably is a chapter on Princess Diana, the queen of hearts. I think back to the day that Magne, Áilu's older reindeer-herding friend, came over and sat with me silently watching the Princess Diana *E! True Hollywood Story* documentary on TV and wonder if there is some sort of cosmic connection between Diana and the reindeer herders of the Arctic. I also cannot help but wonder how this material is relevant or engaging for a bunch of rough and tumble young men, and occasionally young women, who must survive in wild nature and enjoy playing video games in their off time.

Having a school with an area of study particularly focused on reindeer herding is important, and not just for cultural reinforcement. The herders must learn many vital practical topics beyond traditional knowledge: they must learn laws related to herding, about the government institutions that govern their work, as well as rules that must be followed. They must learn the economics of herding, how many reindeer must be sold each year, how to balance this with equipment purchases (such as four wheelers) and other tools. It is a specialized and necessary education.

I prepare a short introduction for my first day with the herders, in Sámi, explaining that I am from America, and go confidently into the classroom and deliver my speech. I then explain, in English, that I want to teach them English because I want them to be able to tell their own stories in the world. It is a classroom of mostly boys and three girls. No reaction, except for an initial eyebrow raise. Many of these kids know me because of Áilu and being in the fence. Most of their parents are my age.

There are no slow claps, as I imagined in the fantasy version of how my first day would unfold. Instead, everyone looks bored or antsy. Someone throws a pencil across the room, hitting one of the other herders squarely. 'Hey, fucker, you stop that!'

Well, there's that. At least some English is spoken. I'll take it as a start.

My other classes are more contained. There are three girls in my *duodji* class, which I teach in the morning. They are eager to learn and I focus on teaching them detailed words related to sewing and handicraft in English. Next come my technical students, an only slightly lower octave of obvious boredom than with the reindeer herders. It is also a class made up of mostly young men and a few girls. A couple sit in the back, a small and slight teenage boy and his not small and slight girlfriend. They spend most of their time holding hands and completely ignoring me.

I'm most intrigued by a Filipino girl – the only foreign student at the school – who sits in the front by the side. Her name is Darna and I know that she's new. She arrived in the Arctic with her mother, who is probably my age, who has married a much older Sámi man. Darna is smart and she pays absolute attention in class. My heart quietly breaks for her because I see her in the halls and during breaks and sitting at lunch all by herself; the other students ignore her. Most of these kids have grown up together from the time they were small children, leaving Darna at an obvious disadvantage. She has a sadness in her eyes. I admire her courage, for all the things she is enduring; I cannot fathom what she is going through, alone in this place in the dead of winter, ignored and away from everything and everyone she knows. I go out of my way to ask how she is, to praise her for her work, to chat when there's time. She is easily becoming one of my favourite students.

The kids just have other things they want to do, other things they care about. The ability to plan for a future is not one of them, a reality typical of most kids every-where. Also, teenagers and hormones – a lethal mix. It's immediately clear why Bradan might have burnt out on teaching: he had a tough audience. It's camaraderie-building when others can see it, too and make light of it, as Viggo often does. Viggo could easily have a PhD in the art of deadpan if one were on offer. One morning before class with the technical students starts, my student couple from the back of the room sit just outside on a bench, engaged in a very public, very explosive make-out session. Viggo walks by to open his classroom door, glances at them and mutters, 'Yeah, that'll last!'

It turns out that Viggo, like most of the other teachers and doctors and foreigners that end up here in municipal jobs, is saving up to travel and for when he's eventually married. Pay is often higher here because of the remote location, and this is the perfect environment for an intro-vert. Viggo is an intellectual: he reads voraciously and can spend days lost in books. He's also a metaphysical seeker: he meditates and studies philosophy and reads books by Alan Watts and Ram Dass. This place gives him permission to be alone.

I am surprised to find, when Viggo has a schedule conflict and asks me to fill in for him for two of his other courses, that he also has the classes with the smartest students, the kids who will end up at university and as teachers and doctors and other professionals. He has them reading great poetry and studying advanced English concepts like metaphors. The kids are vibrant, smart, curious and engaged. I teach them once and wish I could be with them every day. They want to know everything.

I start to wonder if my own students would be more interested in school if they had lessons that were more relevant to them, and so I work on a list of all of the reindeer-herding terms in English: inoculation, castration and on and on. We study the American cowboy, too. In my technical class, knowing that most of the kids will end up working at petrol stations or in garages – and these are enormously important jobs, given that trucks on Arctic routes are carrying vital goods and nearly always driven by foreign drivers, for whom English is the common language after their mother tongue – I start to study lorry parts and tools and start a lesson around their English names, making a game of it by showing pictures of the parts on a projector and having the students guess them out loud. Never did I imagine in this earthly life that I would come to know and be able to identify things like a 'shutter stat' and camshaft. Somewhere along the line, I also remember the first time I saw what may be the longest word in the Sámi language: *guorbmebiilavuoddji*, the word for lorry driver.

School is intense, and exhausting, but I love having a place to which I have to show up every day, as part of something. I especially relish lunchtime, when all the teachers drink coffee together and chat. Everyone is exceedingly nice. Jan Olav, the gym teacher, likes to pull my leg by making up fake Sámi myths, hoping that, like an idiot, I will retell them. The guidance counsellor is an accomplished Sámi poet named Sollaug Sárgon, who has written a book called *Savvon bálgáid luottastit*, meaning 'walk the overgrown path', a title I love to think about when I walk because it describes the nature so perfectly. Solana won't speak English with me; everyone gets me to practise my Sámi in the coffee room, praising me when I get things right.

Bradan, Viggo and a few others do not speak Sámi. One is a soft red-haired woman named Greta; she is Swedish and teaches physics. She has a PhD from Kiruna in the phenomenon of aurora borealis, and it's somehow perfect that she ended up with a reindeer-herder boyfriend in the land of the auroras. And then there's Marit, Áilu's sister-in-law, who is one of the science teachers. I've had virtually no contact with anyone in his family, even though Marit doesn't really count because she and Piera are not in contact with the rest of the family, despite living next door to Áilu's parents. Teaching in the same school gives us an opening to reconnect.

Marit's dog, Čierggis, who was only just recently a puppy herself, has given birth to her first litter, and remembering my fondness for animals, Marit invites me over to the house to see them. Čierggis has had nine puppies, and she lies on her side on cardboard and rags as the tiny furry beans that will become dogs, eyes still closed, struggle blindly over one another to latch on to a teat for milk. These are Lapsk Vallhunds and therefore will make strong and capable reindeer-herding dogs. The males will be adopted quickly, and at a high price, but the futures of the females are less secure, and Marit asks me if I know anyone who wants or needs a puppy.

This absolutely tears at me because I hate how some – but not all – of the people in the village treat dogs, tying them up with blue reindeer rope or making angry posts on the community message board when a poorly fed or constantly restrained dog gets loose or runs free. Tildá, my neighbour, has several medical conditions that make it impossible for her to walk their dog, Guvge, and her lazy teenage son infuriates me because he won't do it, and so Guvge has become a bit like my dog, in that I walk him every chance I get and he often spends the night in my apartment. The cats don't mind at all. Things have gone well with Guvge and I wonder if I should adopt one of the dogs in Marit's new litter. Boo has totally recovered from his Arctic adventure and has spent the winter at home, luxuriating in food served in generous helpings with regularity and sleeping for hours under warm covers. He is settled in.

I decide to adopt one of the female dogs. Marit selects one that is mostly white and with spots of brown and black; she looks like a tiny puffy cotton ball and has the shape of a heart on her head. She won't be able to come home with me for another eight weeks because the puppies need to learn to socialize with other dogs, starting with their siblings, and they need access to their mother's milk and to transition to wet food. I visit every weekend and watch the puppies play and frolic, my puppy looking like a demented but adorable miniature lamb with a tail and milk teeth. Marit's eight-year-old daughter, Malin, takes particular care of my dog, letting her sleep in her room.

I struggle for a name to call my dog. Dogs here are nearly always named after their colour combinations, but because my puppy is white and multicoloured, she largely defies the convention of this naming system. This is also probably why Marit picked her for me: white dogs don't do well in snow-blinding storms, as they can't be seen well in the distance by reindeer herders – you want a black or brown dog for that. My dog was the canine equivalent of misfit produce. But my God, I loved her already.

I want her to have a Sámi name, but one that others could pronounce and remember. She has a heart on her head, and the Sámi word for heart is *váibmu*, which doesn't exactly roll off the tongue. Neither does *násti*, which is the Sámi word for star. I search my Sámi dictionary and settle on Rássi, which means grass or flower. In the teachers' lounge I get some chuckles and guffaws for my name choice, but I explain that I wanted other cultures to be able to say her name. 'This is great,' Viggo says. 'You can run around the village saying "*Grass, grass, where is grass*?"' He doubles over with laughter.

The time comes to bring Rássi home, and even if you don't have a dead mother and abandonment issues, the day you take a puppy away from its mother is one of the hardest days you will ever have with your dog. I bundle Rássi up and walk her home in my arms, promising to take good care of her. It is of some consolation that she'll be able to visit her mother in the future, as we are a short walk away from Marit's house. Rássi cries and whines through the night at the unfamiliarity of it all. But within a week, she is settled for the night, except for my waking her up to go pee outside in the snow every two hours as part of her house-breaking training. I give her the middle name 'Tracy', as a nod to the person in my life that loves animals the most and is a perpetual rescuer of them. After asking her, I also make Tracy the dog godmother, meaning she is the person that would take Boo and Rennie and Rássi if anything were to happen to me. This is something I tell no one in Sápmi for fear of being laughed out of the village. The idea of a dog having a godmother sounds crazy on the surface, but I have a reason beyond my own scars. The number of pets that are put in shelters because of owners who die without a plan and families who don't want to or can't inherit the responsibility is astounding, and I don't want this sort of fate to befall my animals. To that end, I also take out a small life insurance policy and make Tracy the beneficiary, so that in case anything happens to me, she'd be able to get them out of the Arctic and care for them.

It is not what I might have imagined as a young girl in Indiana, but in my own way, I am starting a family.

16

I AM NOT A SÁMI

That spring, I go online and revisit the DNA test I'd taken in New York and what I see gives me pause. A new element of the test result now ascribes levels of confidence to the ancestry breakdown. I still register as almost entirely Northern European, but there is a new distinction between Northern Europe and Scandinavia, with the former now representing low confidence only a tiny slice of my composition. When I first took the test, in the early 2010s, the early days of the technology, I remember seeing a picture of Norway and Sweden with results that showed me to be almost entirely Northern European. Being Northern European doesn't make a person Sámi; something called a haplogroup indicates this information, and my initial result explaining my haplogroup had an accompanying text box about the Sámi. This time when I look more closely at my haplogroup, the genetic population group of people with a common maternal ancestor, I see that my shared links to the Sámi are only partial, putting me on another twig on the same branch of the tree. Reviewing these results, I now see clearly. Am I a Sámi? Absolutely not. Do I share some distant and tangential relation to the Sámi, ages old? Maybe. Sámi people have some shared DNA but they do not all have the same haplogroups.

A local reindeer herder called Hánsa, a Sámi who'd never left our village, had taken a DNA test and found he was Russian. These tests are based on a sampling of data that will only improve its accuracy as more people take them. Sharing some partial and distant DNA certainly does not make anyone part of a culture, and I know this now. I feel a wave of embarrassment for having ever referred to myself as a 'descendant' or having been so excited to think that I had 'found my tribe'. These are simplistic notions, ones that I can now see were based on naivety and overenthusiasm, coupled with a deep desire to have some evidence that I belonged somewhere.

I've learned that DNA means nothing here. You are simply not part of this culture unless people know all of your stories and something about where you came from. Who are your people? Their names? Their immediate history? This is how one belongs: only with context and background. I follow a few Sámi American Facebook groups, members of which are well meaning and earnest, some of whom have grandparents who came to Alaska and Seattle during two of the most significant group migrations to America. They are thrilled to claim their heritage, but I don't think of most of them as Sámi at all: many know little of the culture, the customs or the language. I know for certain the histories of my great-grandparents on my mother's paternal side: my great-grandmother, Clara, was from the West Midlands of England, and my great-grandfather Charles came from the Tyrol, in the Austrian Alps. These were my very direct relatives. But

I know nothing of being British, and I certainly don't speak German or Italian or know what it means to be or feel as one with any of these cultures, despite my known genetic ties. To be part of a culture, you must know its history and be an active part of it. I think of my stepsister Linda, who inherited partial Norwegian ancestry on her father's side, and the way that she lays claim to this affiliation all the time, mentioning attributes that she believes she shares – a Norwegian work ethic, looking Scandinavian – but she has never been to the Nordics and is possibly the least Norwegian person I've ever met in every way, except that she may have used Neutrogena and read Ibsen.

I'd immersed myself in travel and visits because of the belief that I'd found my tribe, and, no matter how misdirected, it was what brought me to exactly where I needed to be in the world exactly when I needed to be there. I also know, more than a year after arriving, that even if I were to suddenly discover that my maternal grandparents were in fact Sámi, it would still *not make me Sámi*. Because I know now that, no matter your background or blood bonds, you simply cannot go home to a place you've never been. Your lived culture makes you who you are. I speak the language poorly and have no history in Kautokeino; I do not share stories or understanding or cultural norms. I think about a magazine article I'd written earlier based on my time in the Arctic, which reflected what I understood and believed to be true at the time. What now makes me cringe is the last sentence of the article: 'I am Sámi.' Because I am not a Sámi; I am also not English or Irish or French or any of the other things the test thinks I can be with its constantly evolving veracity. I am a Midwesterner from Indiana who can tell you anything you want to know about thunderstorms and corn and late-night-television host David Letterman. But for a variety of reasons, I am not a Sámi.

*

In some ways, Rássi has made me whole, given me confidence. I'm now out and about all the time. She's still tiny but we walk together everywhere over the tundra, lit up in rapidly melting blinding white by the sun. There is a large bank of rocks about half a kilometre from my house, facing a farmer's field. Leading up to it is a foot path that passes a natural spring that gurgles in the melting snow, running parallel with part of the path. Gerlinde makes displays for museums and does costuming for historical indigenous TV and local theatre productions, and is a font of traditional indigenous knowledge. She too was with a reindeer herder before Bernt Morten. She teaches me the importance of the spring, both for water and for spiritual reasons; every time I pass it I give it thanks. I sit Rássi on one of the big rocks in the embankment and take her picture; I name the rock Rássi rock. It's a rock that needed a name, because it's a place I would always go to pray and meditate when things were feeling out of sorts. Now it's also where I go to mark Rássi's growth.

One day behind the rocks, I catch a glimpse of a red fox in terrible condition, patches of fur falling off it in clumps. I know right away that the fox has sarcoptic mange and is probably in a great deal of pain. The mange spreads, so I also know it's important that the animal be put down right away: it looked to be suffering greatly and near death. What I don't know is how to find the person who has permission to shoot the fox – this is tightly regulated in the north. I scoop Rássi up and take her home, and first call to a vet in Alta, who tells me to call the local Kautokeino police station. I'm worried that the fox will move and I'll be unable to find it, and I am impatient to reach someone. The Sámi police clerk answers, and I tell her in Sámi that I have found a fox, except it hits me, only after dialling, that I do not know how to say the word fox in Sámi. She answers in English.

'We are the police, we do not have a fax,' she says.

'No, I have found a fox,' I say, all in Sámi except for the word *fox*, again.

She once again replies in English. 'There is no fax machine here. We have no fax. There is no fax here.'

I'm struggling to make myself understood. I come close to singing out the annoying Norwegian dance song 'What Does the Fox Say' but stop myself short. One more time I say 'fox' and she replies for the last time, exasperated, 'No fax is here!'

All the while, the phone is cradled in my arm and I'm searching frantically in the bookshelves for my elementary flash cards or one of my Sámi children's picture books, which I'm certain has a picture of a fox with the proper name. I find it.

'*Rieban!*'

The woman understands, and we both laugh heartily at the miscommunication. I learn how to say *rieban* properly, and she learns the English word *fox*.

She calls a man with a shotgun, and he comes right away, meeting me at the edge of the path. I must lead him to the fox, which we find easily. It is cowering between the rocks, in extreme distress. Its death is quick and clean, taken with one shot, but as with everything else I've watched die first-hand, I mourn the fox and its end. Experiencing the cycle of life and death is always awful. But this is life here. This is living in nature.

School is clipping along; I'm in a routine with my teaching but also fearing that I'm a bit of a drain on Viggo because my Norwegian is extremely poor. My daily life at this point is conducted in Norwegian, of course – on food labels in the grocery store, in online banking and in other small daily transactions – but this is all based on understanding very general Norwegian, which is not terribly difficult as an English speaker. The school operating system – where attendance and grades are marked – is also in Norwegian, but the words used are not common or to be found in dictionaries or Google Translate. Therefore, Viggo needs to spend an endless amount of time, on top of his school load, taking me through the system as I input grades and mark attendance. When there are school administration meetings with all of the teachers, I'm also at a loss. These meetings are held in Norwegian because there are so many non-Sámi teachers at the school, and I have no idea what anyone is saying. I make do the best I can, but there are layers of things I know I am missing.

Greta, with the PhD in auroras, is becoming a friend. She's extremely bright and I feel a kinship with her, in that she moved here to be with a reindeer herder, experiencing everything as an outsider in much the same way I had. Her mother had died a few years prior, and except for a brother in Stockholm, she is on her own here. She comes to my place for coffee and we take long walks with our dogs; we make each other laugh. Greta and her boyfriend invite me to come to their summer pasture, where the reindeer from their district must be marked; spring is birthing season. It is July and school is out for the summer.

I have the option of walking to the summer pasture, which is something that the older people still sometimes do. It's thirty kilometres or so and takes from dawn to dusk with steady walking. There are no roads, and if not walking, it's necessary to take an ATV over the rough landscape. I would've liked to walk, had it not been for two important considerations: Rássi was still small and the distance would have been too long for her; and I have a terrible sense of direction and could easily imagine myself accidentally ending up in Finland. This is not a place where there is cellular coverage so smartphones won't work. Instead, we make a plan: I will get a ride to the end of the road in Kautokeino to the west, forty kilo-metres away, near an abandoned gold and copper mine called Bidjovaggi. Greta will come on the ATV and pick us up from there.

I pack a very large backpack with only the essen-tials: sweatshirts and changes of woollen socks and underwear. A neighbour drops me near the mine. Greta appears on the ATV splattered in mud, her red hair in a long braid, face sunburned. I attempt to hold Rássi on the ATV but she will have none of it, wrangling herself off to run beside us as we bounce across the rugged landscape, filled with rocks and streams. Rássi is a reindeer-herd-ing dog through and through, and she flies filled with purpose. I'm astonished by Greta's dexterity, navigating the difficult terrain with me on the back. We climb steep hills and, after a few hours, come to the area for their herding district, high in the mountains, and then arrive at Greta's and her boyfriend's cabin, a small and austere one-room wooden structure with some simple beds, a table and chairs and a small hob for cooking. There is an outhouse next door and another down the hill, for more … involved toilet visits.

The sun is up almost constantly, and there is work to be done; we wait for the herders to bring the reindeer and their calves into the enclosures. With an almost-ever-present sun, and the lingering halo of light from the sunset, the typical punctuations of time and daily life do not exist; the schedule is sleep briefly, wake up, work, eat, sleep briefly and repeat, on a full twenty-four-hour cycle.

The herders collect the calves and bring them into an enclosure. Inside, we put large loose rubber bands with plastic number cards around the necks of the calves, and the numbers are called out. Owners identify the calves from their reindeer and the calves are then marked on the ear with each herder's individual mark. This is done with a knife in a series of quick cuts to cause a minimum of pain to the animal. Once the calves are marked, they are let out again, and, miraculously, most know to find their own mothers in another enclosure. There are those that do not, and you can hear their cries, which kills me, as you might expect.

There are a couple of days' rest, when the next batch of reindeer have not yet come in. We take the short hike down to the cabin of Greta's boyfriend's family; I know his mother, May, and his sister, Inger Marie. May is making a giant pot of fish stew out of fresh Arctic char that have just been caught nearby; the fish is delicious and fresh and clean, its pink flesh meaty and satiating with no ingredients save a touch of salt. May does not speak a lick of English and tests me on my Sámi, which remains terrible. She wants to know if I have a boyfriend yet. Of course, I do not.

We walk with a water jug to a spring to collect water, and also to the local refrigerator, which is actually the last patch of snow with a deep hole in it, covered by a heavy rug. We pick up sausages and some hard cheese and head back to the cabin. Greta's boyfriend, Ole, has been working for hours on his ATV, which has broken down, making him unable to travel out with the others to collect the next batch of reindeer for marking. He's given up out of frustration, and the others have left him behind. Another herder not tasked with driving the reindeer appears with a giant flask of Wild Turkey, and then another friend shows up, and everyone is drinking. Greta and I stick to wine. Someone radios in that the reindeer will come in a few hours; her boyfriend is at this point in no condition to mark the calves, but they still need to be marked. Greta looks to one of Ole's older cousins, who is sitting at the kitchen table, and suddenly she pulls out a stack of paper plates and a knife and instructs the cousin, in Norwegian, to show her Ole's mark using the plate. She practises over and over, making the intricate grooves into paper plates as quickly as she can. Ole is asleep when the reindeer are driven in, and I am astonished when Greta goes in to the fence and does all of the marking for that day by herself. I think she's one of the most amazing people I've ever met.

After some days, I need to get back to the apartment to take care of the cats; I've left Tildá feeding them. One of Ole's young cousins agrees to drive me down the mountain with Rássi, who mostly runs beside us. We get home and I have the most gratifying shower of my life, layers of dirt and earth and reindeer fur coming off of me. There is nothing like a shower after not having one for several days. Rássi crawls under the bed and sleeps for almost twenty-four hours straight, ready for her next adventure.

17

LONDON

Out of the blue, I get a call from an old work acquaintance in London that I hadn't heard from in years. He needs a partner for a media-consulting project. We put together a proposal and I'm asked to travel to London to give a presentation pitch for the work. I scramble to find someone to take care of the animals; I end up asking Tildá to come down each day to feed the cats, to which she happily agrees, and decide to leave Rássi with Viggo, who is responsible and, it also seems, would benefit from some company. He's renting a generously sized top half of a house now, in the town centre, just across from the school, so he'll also be able to run home to give Rássi toilet breaks during the day.

It's been so long since I've had to wear anything but snow pants or fleeces, I'm at a loss as to what I would now wear in the city – most of my nice clothes are still in a storage area in New York, along with nearly everything else I own. I take the bus to Alta and buy some cheap black trousers and a blouse at H&M and pack them along with a single pair of high heels, thankful that I saved this pair from the fire, back in the time of my first winter alone, when I'd not yet known how to get firewood.

Not counting a quick trip or two down south to Oslo for a couple of days at most, I'd not been in a major city for more than two years. When I arrive at my luxury hotel in London, I revel in the French milled soap and tiny bottles of shampoo and body lotion, the gushing showerhead and the ready availability of cappuccinos at Pret A Mangers on nearly every corner. In Kautokeino, the only place to get a cappuccino was at the Statoil, out of a vending machine. I catch myself in the floor-length hotel mirror – another thing I did not have at home – and see how wild and unkempt I've become: long and split-ended hair, home coloured from a box into a veritable plethora of shades of streaky yellow; unruly eyebrows; and clothing that smelled distinctly like the basement must of my apartment.

We take the meeting and win the project work, and I'm left with a couple of days to wander around London. I first go to the Victoria and Albert Museum, and buy a small notebook and sit staring at the exhibits for hours, writing down my impressions as if I had never actually been in a museum before. The treasures stun me: sculptures by Bernini and Canova, the ancient artwork, feats of human creativity that utterly mesmerize me in their complexity and detail. There is nothing like this in Kautokeino, and being away from art has vastly sharpened my appreciation of it to a point that I've never experienced at such a deep level before; it feels emotional and profound, awe-inspiring.

I equally love walking down the bustling streets of

London, amazed by the numbers and types of restaurants. *A shop dedicated to grilled cheese! A fried chicken shop!* Deciding that I should stock up on some things I can't find in Norway, I make my way to Kensington High Street and the Whole Foods grocery market, a store that had been a favourite of mine in America. I want to pick up some staples like proper peanut butter and green tea, and spices that I've not been able to find in the north, or simply don't know the names for in Norwegian, like cumin.

When I'm in the store, something strange happens. I take the escalator downstairs and turn a corner to see a table piled high with eggs. Eggs of every colour – blue, brown, white – all with names: *Marans* and *Buff Orpingtons* and *Anconas*. Who ever knew there could be so many types of eggs in the world? I'm overcome by the sheer volume of choice. It's too much. I become dizzy and I burst into tears, right in the middle of the store. In the north, I've been with so little of this level of choice – excessive, really – that it stops me cold and takes my breath away, and not in a good way. I'm flooded with overwhelming thoughts, starting with the crashing realization of how much of my life had been subconsciously focused on the pursuit of money to have access to things like those on offer in a store like this, the gluttonous variety of choice and the endless cycle of consumption it inspired. I look at the meat counter and the mountains of specialty cheeses and the piles of seafood and think about all the things that will spoil or go to waste because there is no way that all of these things will be sold. Living things were killed for this immense array, and the excess makes me physically ill. I leave without my peanut butter, knocked into an existential crisis.

This is the moment that I'm struck by how much I've changed. I've moved between two worlds, my internal compass reset to the point that having and acquiring things has become so much less important. I've now lived with so much less, out of necessity and by virtue of geography, that I've come to recognize how little these things matter. I look back at my old self and see someone who was selfish and indulgent, really, living for the accumulation of things. Living with less and living in the heart of nature, without distraction, has also developed my sensitivity to the fact that I am a small but active part of the grand machine that is the natural environment, and my decisions and my ways of being in the world have impacts and ripple effects; everything is sublimely connected. It's as if I was deaf to this truth in New York, and perhaps for my whole life, before arriving in the north.

*

July in Norway is the month in which everyone takes off for vacation. Kautokeino is no exception. Marit and Piera are going to the south with their five kids and need someone to look after their dogs: Rássi's mother, Čierggis, and her grandfather, Vilge, as well as an uncle of Rássi's of the same age, a cream-coloured puppy named Guvge, just like Tildá's dog. They ask if I will look after them and I happily agree, which means walking over every morning to feed the dogs and let them out, then bringing them into the house at night. Rássi is thrilled to be around her literal family of dogs, bounding and tearing around the yard until she becomes exhausted. Dogs are always running amok in Kauto, and a couple of other random neighbours start to show up every day as well, leaving me with an actual gang of dogs who run and chase each other for hours. I indulge them with copious numbers of dried pig ears and fresh meat, knowing that they won't get to eat like this when Marit and Piera return, because people simply don't feed dogs this way here. I could watch these dogs for hours, and that's exactly what I do, sitting on a stoop in the sun as they run around the yard, littered with broken snowmobiles and an old tractor and kids' toys.

One day, out of nowhere, Áilu appears to say hello. It's not unusual in that his parents live next door, but I am unprepared to see him, and the first thing I notice is that he's wearing a gold wedding ring on his finger. It's been more than two years, but I'm still stunned all the same.

'You're married?' I ask him.

'No, no, I am not married.' He shakes his head. 'How are you doing?' he asks.

I respond curtly, telling him I'm fine. I don't want to talk to him and wish he'd leave. I don't want to be back with Áilu, but I do have a deep sense of hurt about his being with someone else. I wanted to believe that when we broke up it was because he needed to live the life of a reindeer herder and not be attached to anyone. But apparently this was just a story I'd told myself to blunt the plain fact that he simply did not want to be with me.

I also wonder why, with a wedding band plainly on his finger, he would bother to lie and tell me that he wasn't married. This bothered me excessively, until a Norwegian friend told me that a band is often worn by both males and females on the occasion of an engagement.

I take Rássi camping; twenty-four-hour sun is amazing for this, in that it's never dark so you needn't worry about lighting fires to see or things that go bump in the night. Also, virtually nothing on land in the north can kill you in summer. There are no poisonous snakes or giant bears lurking to attack. I have a car now, and so we take a road trip. The local car-rental guy, Johan, had sold me one of his older cars, a metallic green 2004 Škoda Octavia station wagon, for next to nothing. After two years of walking everywhere through the Arctic and begging rides, it's like a dream to be able to get in the car and go, crossing over to Finland for cheaper groceries or making the drive to Karasjok to visit Stein, which I often do with Rássi, sleeping in the back room of the newspaper office, where there is a fold-out bed for visitors. I pack a tent and Rássi and I drive through Alta and along the northern coast, passing through astonishing wide-open mountains which slope dramatically on either side, cutting through the kommune of Kvalsund and past a large village called Skaidi and through Stabbursdalen, known for its world-class salmon fishing, and then Lakselv, where Stein was born. We camp at night, stopping one evening to visit Stein at a friend's summer cabin, before passing on to Karasjok and then back up to Kautokeino on the *vidda*, effectively having done a giant loop through the north.

My consulting work has started to take me back and forth from Kautokeino more and more, and my teaching contract wasn't renewed, which was not a huge loss or even a surprise; I expected the job to be temporary, and I couldn't travel and continue teaching. Ellen Inga had thanked me graciously for my work and gave me a Sámi coffee pouch at a group meeting in the teachers' lounge, telling me that she'd call me back when substitutes were needed. The consulting work was life-saving, in that through it I was making good money now and able to easily pay my bills, which had been a constant and unending stressor in my life.

I work and I walk Rássi; we now have a new favourite route, one that goes down a road that I affectionately refer to as 'airport road' because it leads straight to a giant clearing of dirt in which pontoon planes and the occasional helicopter land. The road to the 'airport' is flanked by vast swaths of tundra, and to the right-hand side, headed west, a huge one-kilometre track for reindeer racing in the wintertime. I walk down airport road frequently with Greta and our dogs, and most especially enjoy the walk if there is a storm approaching; weather changes in an instant in the north, and it is not every year that there are thunderstorms, but when they come, they are magnificent and arresting. Light-blue skies give way to ever-darkening clouds of Aegean blue that you can see rolling forward, like ink slowly spilling out of a jar onto cloth, until the whole sky becomes dark, as if preparing a canvas for the dramatic dance of lightning strikes that come down in unpredictable jagged sizzles. I know thunderstorms are dangerous – of course I know this – but there is something about being amid the raw power of nature unleashed that enchants me. As kids in Indiana, we were taught to gauge the distance of a thunderstorm by slowly reciting 'one Mississippi, two Mississippi, three Mississippi' and so on, starting the recitation with the lightning strike and continuing the count until thunder could be heard. The number of Mississippis recited was meant to tell you how many miles away the storm was. I was never sure if this was a reliable gauge, but I was also never struck by lightning.

I spend so much time outside that I feel amiss if I skip even one walk. In many ways, it's healed me and has become my form of meditation. My anxiety and OCD have been terrible personal handicaps with which I've struggled mightily throughout my life – constantly worried, constantly concerned about making a mistake. I knew that this had mostly logical origins and stemmed from childhood and always having to be ready for what my primal brain perceived as danger or attack: being judged or accused, worrying at all times about being sent away. Over time, these reactions became baked into my personality and part of who I am. It is an exhausting way to live. I know well how my mind works: one problem assuaged and I head straight to something else to fill its place and worry over. Nature somehow tamped down these impulses. By contrast, in New York I'd go to great lengths to consult doctors and find external solutions for these behaviours, even at one point being prescribed Adderall, the medication for people with ADHD. Because of the stimulant effect, it was basically like taking cocaine and it had a terrible effect on my anxiety and OCD. I would become jittery and sharp and wired, hyper-focused and unable to turn it all off, the feeling so intense that I would have to take something to sleep. I had such a negative reaction that I ultimately ended up flushing it down the toilet, never wanting to be so controlled by a medicine again. Now I am in a wholly unintended rhythm of calming myself through these long walks, surrounded by nature. In nature I am finding time to quiet the racing thoughts in my head, and to pray, and reflect. It is becoming an essential part of my life, and I cannot walk through the woods without feeling an extraordinary gratitude for the healing I feel, and a level of calmness and peace I never imagined possible.

Aside from Greta's visits, people don't come over much, but I like to go upstairs and chat with Tildá when I'm feeling social or in need of company. We sit in her cluttered living room while she works on her Sámi handicraft. Tildá is always working on something, from purses to fishing lines to carvings; she has a talent for this kind of work. Visitors are always popping in and out; she seems to be a friend and mentor to many of the young adults in the village who like to come and talk through their problems and get advice. They come to her because she's lived a difficult life, and more importantly, she is kind and non-judgemental. Bjarne often comes by for a coffee after finishing his shift at the petrol station, and he's become a friend of mine as well. The thing I appreciate most about Bjarne is his absolute kindness; he loves Tildá's dog, Guvge, as much as I do, and all animals in a way that is not common here. He also always helps anyone he can, from Tildá to anyone else in the village who might be experiencing any number of small crises from needing a jump-start for a dead battery or getting stuck in a snowdrift. Rássi loves Bjarne, and Bjarne can always make Rássi come back when she's run away. I simply yell, 'Bjarne, bacon,' Rássi's two favourite words, and she is sure to come back. Always.

Bjarne's wife, Maia, is a mystery to me. She's a Sámi woman from the neighbouring village of Ávži and she works in the local kommune, doing important administrative work, including translation. I see her around the village occasionally, at the market with Bjarne or walking up and down the main road. I would like to know her better, and I suggest to Bjarne that his entire family come over at some point – he also has two kids, a girl and a boy. I would like to know all of them better.

One day while we are drinking coffee Tildá shares some disappointing news. She's moving. A house has become available to rent one street over, on Heargedievvá, which in Sámi means reindeer hill. The house has two bedrooms and a basement and a very large yard. The move will be good for Tildá: she has a teenage son at home and another son who visits frequently. She is a lovely woman but a classic packrat, and I wonder how she's going to get everything out of the apartment and into her new place.

*

After several delays, my master's programme is finally ready to start. I am outside the university cafeteria during orientation when I hear a loud voice chattering above the rest, peppering conversation with a generous number of insertions of 'like', 'you know' and 'oh wow'. My mind cannot place the accent at first, but it's deeply familiar to me. She is so loud.

'My perfect Arctic silence has been shattered,' I write in my journal.

Rachel, an American from California, is in my master's programme, and in odds that might rival winning the lottery, she even attended the same undergraduate university in America I'd attended. We are both now in the Arctic. Her bubbly enthusiasm, loud laughter and immediate and imposed familiarity with others grates on me in a way that is visceral, surprising and even shameful in its unkindness. As my classmates introduce themselves, I half listen as my mind races to figure out why I am being so judgey and, frankly, awful in my attitude. It occurs to me only later that Rachel bothers me so much because I recognize myself, albeit some years earlier, newly arrived in the Arctic, nervous, chatty, looking in all directions for points of connection and acceptance in a world unknown.

We can never read each other's minds, but I believe Rachel to be deeply disappointed to discover that she is not the only American in this part of the world. I infer this when I hear her story, and about her travels around the Middle East and other exotic environs. I judge Rachel immediately to be one of these insufferable twenty-something Instagrammers who travel to exotic locales and take pictures of themselves for no other reasons than to show that they can and they have. My opinion of her drops further when I troll her Instagram account and see that she's posted a provocative semi-nude shot of herself in the university sauna, replete with a shadow of naked boobs and a cascade of hair.

Rachel additionally hits a nerve when describing her background and life experience, bragging that she'd organized a local version of a symposium that was part of a bigger conference; it was the same organization for which I'd been head of global media for a number of years. Rachel just seemed to serve as a catalyst for bubbling forth a host of negative feelings. Why did I even care? I had no answers within easy reach beyond that Rachel, in part, represented a living, breathing facsimile of my old self.

The master's programme in Sámi journalism had initially been conceived to foster a new generation of highly trained Sámi journalists and help develop their skills. The idea was bold and forward thinking – in any indigenous community seeking to strengthen itself, institutions that reflect the culture are essential because they are often vastly different from those of majority societies. Knowing how to reconcile professional reporting demands and indigenous concerns was an area ripe for development and exploration. What is shared and what is not shared in the course of an interview, for example, becomes important in indigenous reporting. Respecting traditions and ways of being is also important. Because I spoke English, I could not keep count of the number of times majority media reporters had contacted me to ask about how to pursue stories in the Arctic, such as wanting to write about Sámi shamans (something not publicly discussed). Film crews would call with dates of arrival, expecting that reindeer herders would immediately take them up on the *vidda* to cover them working, which is not possible because the animals and nature work on a schedule of their own, not that of a production company. Herding is a tough and dangerous job, and almost no reindeer herder would take a camera crew with them in the middle of work. The request was insulting in its lack of understanding or consideration.

The journalism programme had sought to strengthen Sámi journalism, but at some point the decision was taken to expand it to not only Sámi journalists but anyone interested in indigenous concerns and the wider issues in reporting on indigenous cultures. And in a first for the university, the programme would be taught in English, the common language of the first cohort.

The students are from the Netherlands, Brazil, Kenya and Finland. There are two Sámis: Liv Inger, a highly

respected Sámi journalist, and a reindeer-herder journalist from Finland. Our professors, academics who
conceived the programme with the idea of getting it off
the ground and then handing it over to the Sámi administration after a couple of years, are from the UK and
Finland and will fly in for blocks at a time to teach. All
of the students are in their twenties and thirties, save for
Liv Inger and myself, the old ladies of the group, in our
fifties and forties respectively.

Everyone, save for Liv Inger, lives nearby so I decide
to have them all over one evening, professors included,
so that we can get to know each other better. I order reindeer pizza from the local pizza place, Pit Stop, and we
sit and talk in my apartment. The young woman from
Kenya, Layla, is terrified of dogs, but Rássi is one of the
world's cutest puppies, and naturally, as dogs are wont to
do, she heads straight for Layla, jumping on her to give
her kisses as if to reassure her that dogs can be loving and
kind. Layla's obvious fear evaporates before our eyes, and
Rássi sits firmly on her lap the rest of the evening. Layla
takes pictures of herself with Rássi and emails them to
her parents, who are astounded. The evening somehow
concludes with everyone doing the limbo in my living
room using a broom – led by the sixty-something Finnish
professor, who had started the evening stony faced and
quiet and had utterly transformed.

The evening expedites our familiarity – I genuinely
like everyone in my class, and am even starting to warm
to Rachel, seeing now, regrettably, that years of condi-
tioning, developed before I'd arrived in the Arctic, have
led me to often reflexively assess everyone and everything, coming down with a judgement on people and

situations, needing to have an answer about where they fit. This kind of thinking has never served me, and in fact has limited me in the ability to let life happen. It's exhausting having to live in a constant state of defensive evaluation, and as with all things that come with only time in the north, from good friendships to the twenty-four-hour sun, I am slowly learning that sometimes the greatest gifts are to be discovered in letting things unfold. Wonderful things are waiting to be revealed.

18

ČÁHPPE

Early one evening in the dead of winter, I'm at the Rema 1000 grocery on the other side of town, when two of the master's programme students, Lieuwe and Camila, enter the store, both looking badly shaken. I ask Lieuwe what's wrong.

'Near the bridge, a black dog was badly hit by a car.'

'Is it still there?'

'No. A guy in a big blue truck picked it up, put it in the passenger seat with him and drove away quickly. It was so much blood,' Lieuwe says, in a sort of stunned shock.

I feel like I've been stomach punched with a bowling ball. I don't need more information to know who this was, between the colour of the dog and the description of the truck. This was Áilu's dog, Čáhppe. My wonderful Čáhppe, who long after Áilu left would regularly come to the apartment to check on me, and who would sit outside of my window, and sometimes follow me with Rássi on walks when he wasn't out reindeer herding with Áilu. Áilu truly loves this dog. I love this dog.

I try to call Áilu but I can't get through, and so I contact Marit, who confirms that it was Čáhppe. The injuries were too profound for survival; the nearest vet was two hours away and he would not have stood a chance. Áilu did not have the heart to kill Čáhppe by his own hand, and so Piera had to put him out of his misery, quickly shooting him.

Those of us that love animals do so because they love unconditionally and ask for so little in return. Čáhppe had been my friend and my teacher here in the north. We had literally travelled many miles together. I look at the sky and it's as if the whole world is marking his passage from this world to the next.

I write in my journal.

Čáhppe I love you so.
The northern lights flew over the village.
Even the moon was red.
I love you.
I will never forget you.

*

Another Christmas is approaching. I will spend it on my own with Rássi and, of course, the cats. I love the Christmas season; stoking my black cast-iron stove in which I make roaring fires; the electric Scandinavian Christmas lights, made to look like seven burning candles, put in the windows of every house; the specialty foods that only come out now. I put a festive red and white duvet on the bed and pull out my exceedingly tacky but beloved Santa Claus oilcloth for the kitchen table. I even have a fake Christmas tree, which Rennie and Boo love to sleep under. I've decorated it with pretty paper ornaments from Juhls' and white twinkly Christmas lights.

Tildá notices that I am alone and invites me for a traditional Norwegian dinner on Christmas Eve: *lutefisk* – cod cured in lye (as delicious as it sounds to a non-Norwegian, by the way!); *ribbe* – bits of crispy pork belly; and dried lamb called *pinnekjøtt*. I go to church and sit in the back; the service is in Sámi and Norwegian, and I like to sing along to the hymns, watching people come in wearing their *gákti* in all its finery. We have a lovely and peaceful Christmas on our own, just me and the animals. As usual, I don't hear anything from my family, save for the gift of some holiday money sent by my dad and for which I'm always grateful. But the lack of contact or any delivering of holiday cheer has been the norm for longer than I can remember. I have spent more Christmases alone at this point in my life than with my family. There were times that this would have ripped me apart, but now I just feel resigned to the reality, because it's not likely to ever change.

Once the holidays are over, our schedules are free and I finally have the chance to invite Bjarne and Maia over with their kids. I make American chili, but with reindeer mince, and have to get the shredded cheddar cheese in Finland. As we sit chatting, we race from topic to topic with ease, and I wonder how so much time has passed here without having met Maia. I love her. She is one of the smartest people I've encountered, and not just in Kautokeino. She is able to explain so much about the history of the area, the families and the state of local and national politics. She's thoughtful and welcomes a good debate. And like Bjarne, she also has a good heart. She is open and welcoming, funny even, with an incredible gift for deadpan, which she has passed on to her teenage daughter, Sunna Mari, a beautiful girl with glasses, milky white skin and a thick mane of chestnut hair, who sits silently and attentively absorbing everything around her, as if sizing things up, occasionally chiming in with an astute comment or two. Bjarne doesn't speak Sámi, as his wife and kids do, but the whole family speaks perfect English, which is a huge relief to me. Nils Åke, the son, has an impressive knowledge of riddles, also delivered in English, and he peppers us with them through the evening. I also learn that Maia is a dedicated litter picker, which thrills me, because I spend hours and hours picking up trash on the tundra and on the roadsides, and I'm happy to know that I'm not alone in this behaviour, which I like to regard as the highest use of my OCD cleaning compulsion. I make a mental note to connect her with Gerlinde, who is also constantly picking up trash, and has even gone so far as to create a daily Facebook post sarcastically called 'catch of the day', which, instead of fish, features pictures of the assorted garbage she has picked out of nature, from empty cigarette boxes to straws and Styrofoam food containers and the dreaded blue plastic rope fragments used by reindeer herders and, unfortunately, found everywhere, embedded in the dirt and tangled in the brush.

No one in their right mind ever tosses away cans and plastic bottles, though; they are worth several kroner a piece in Norway, easily exchanged in the grocery store at machines which eat the cans and spit out a receipt for cash or store credit. You can even donate the money. When I was first alone in Kautokeino, in the warmer months, I would earn extra money by going to the football field early in the morning, when no one could see me, and collecting all the cans and sports drink bottles littering the field from the night before. I would sometimes make as much as £20 a day by just picking up cans and bottles. We now occasionally have unofficial contests to see who can pick up the weirdest trash: one very early misty morning while walking Rássi, I stumble on a torn pair of pantyhose, one high-heeled shoe and a bottle of vodka on the path, stuck in the underbrush. Even trash can tell a story.

We have one of the coldest winters on record, with many days of minus forty or below. Minus forty is also the temperature at which Celsius and Fahrenheit become one and the same. There are outlets for cars everywhere in the village and outside of homes, even my apartment building, as it's necessary to plug one's car in using a special cord every night so the engine is kept warm enough to start in the morning. My Škoda is a Czech car, a diesel, and a veritable tank in the winter, able to start in the most challenging of conditions, which is why there are so many of them in the north. It's waiting for the ice to melt off the front and rear windshields enough to drive that presents the problem. It is so deep and stubborn that merely scraping it isn't enough: you scrape the glass as best you can, then turn the car on with the heater on full blast so that the ice will melt, run inside and have a quick cup of coffee before going outside to scrape again.

Despite the cold, Rássi still needs to go for regular pees and poops outside, and so I must bundle up to take her on walks. In these temperatures, eyelashes freeze in an instant, and the air is sharp to breathe. Warm feet and covered hands are the keys to keeping warm in massively sub-zero temperatures; when it's cold and dry, I wear my *gápmagat*, handmade reindeer skin boots with curled toes, lined with heavy wool inserts and worn with thick wool socks, which wick the moisture and keep feet dry. Nothing else will do. I wear the gloves that herders often wear when driving their snowmobiles in the mountains in these temperatures: long sleeve-like waterproof mittens, filled with fleece, that go up to the elbows, theirs worn atop thick winter duster coats. I don't have wind chill to worry about as much, so I simply wear my thick jacket. As long as she's able to keep moving, Rássi is fine in the cold for short spurts. She is, after all, an Arctic dog.

But when the temperature drops, I often notice stray dogs wandering at night, and no animal should tolerate minus forty and below. Many can't. I bring them inside, always. I never know how these dogs will react with Rennie and Boo, so instead of bringing them in to the main part of the apartment, I line my foyer with blankets and set out food and water, closing the door that leads to the rest of the rooms, so that they will have warmth and shelter, while protecting the cats from harm. Two dogs come frequently. One has the long ears and funny fur eyebrow marks that many Sámi dogs have, leading most of them to be named Čalbmi, meaning 'eyes'. The other is a bit of a mutt, short haired, unlike the other dogs in the Arctic, mostly brown with black spots and a tattered collar. He comes to my house the most. The dogs usually run home in the morning, and I only bring them in if it's late at night. If they stay, I post their picture in the lost dog group on Facebook, and the owners usually collect them summarily. But the brown dog returns again and again, leaving during the day and returning at least one or two nights a week, and then away for long stretches. I wonder to whom he belongs.

In late winter, a work project that I'd dedicated myself to almost exclusively for the past couple of years abruptly and unexpectedly hits a major snag, and there is a disagreement over my contract. I lose my salary almost overnight and am thrown into worry about what will happen next. This is always a potential risk when working as a consultant, and up until now, I've been lucky to not have had anything like this happen. But it brought back old feelings of anxiety, which overwhelm me, happening just as I was settling into a rhythm.

In times of extreme ambiguity, I've never shied away from sources of good advice, including a couple of well-respected psychics. One is a woman in California named Louise, who I've been talking to once a year for at least fifteen years. She has made some astonishing predictions since I've known her, and I have long been convinced of her sincerity and her accuracy, a trust built over time. And there is a friend of one of my best friends, named Pattie, who is a straight talking psychic from New York who's given me a couple of readings and is more like a therapist. A good psychic can't tell you everything that will happen in your future, but they can tell you what is meant to be revealed to you, using their own language and their own interpretations. Good psychics can't tell you lotto numbers or other ridiculous things. They can't drive your destiny or influence outcomes or do any of the things bad ones claim to be able to do, therefore giving real psychics and intuitives a bad name. They're also usually terrible at timing, because if you ask any good psychic, they're relaying information that lives outside of time. In my own analogy, I think of them as God's stenographers: they are simply passing on need-to-know messages. Over time, depending on the situation, I have come to view Louise and Pattie as important spiritual counsellors and friends. They don't give just straight predictions; they gave something more, which is often bigger themes around what is happening and why, from a spiritual perspective.

The fact that I consult psychics at all is not something I could share with everyone, at the risk of someone labelling me flighty or gullible. I am neither of these things. But I am also often surrounded by sceptics who are quick to dismiss anything they cannot explain entirely using the scientific method, and I find that way of thinking to be both restrictive and incredibly narcissistic – who could possibly have an ego big enough to believe that they had the universe and its mysterious workings figured out with absolute certainty?

I call Pattie to say I have a question about a work situation. I am silent as she tells me that she doesn't think things will end quickly, but that I must hold on.

19

ELLOS (LIFE)

We're having a particularly warm early summer. It always amazes me that the Arctic can be forty below and colder, but when summer comes around, the temperatures can rise to as much as seventy degrees Fahrenheit. This summer is turning out to be unseasonably warm, and I take Rássi over to Marit's for a visit, where I find her sitting on their deck, sunning herself. On the way, we pass by Stine's old house, which has activity around it and looks as if it's been sold. I'd emailed Stine a few times and never got responses, but seeing the house and the swing set that still remained in front reminded me of her and the kids and how much I missed them. As we sit and have coffee I ask Marit if she'd heard any news of Stine.

Marit sits up and opens her eyes. 'Oh, terrible story. You did not hear what happened?'

'No? What?'

'The small one, Mikkel Sebastian, took ill with a fever down south. He died after a short illness, only two weeks or so. Very sudden,' she says, shaking her head slowly. 'Only two and a half years old.'

I can hardly believe it. I go home and email Stine, telling her how sorry I am for her loss, asking if there is anything I can do. She writes back a couple of days later. 'I lost my son. How do you think I am? I need time.' I can't pretend to remotely understand the depth of her sorrow. A memory that sits with me is the day of my sister's funeral, and catching a glimpse of my father standing alone, after everyone had left, looking down at Anna in her casket to say goodbye for the last time. I'd never seen my father, a tall, vigorous pillar of strength, cry before, but I watched him touching her hand, quietly sobbing. My father lost a part of himself that day, and would often say in later years that there was nothing worse than losing a child. I did not email Stine again; I wanted to respect her and give her the space she needed to grieve.

I'm seeing Marit and Piera together at the house less and less. Marit has been lightly grumbling, when we are alone, that she is getting tired of Kautokeino. She feels that her kids need the bigger opportunities of the south, and she'd like for them all to move down to Trondheim, where she's from. It turns out that their previous summer trip had been to encourage Piera to warm to the idea. But he was a reindeer herder, and to some degree, even I knew this was wishful thinking. People don't generally confide in each other regarding personal situations here, but I suspected this was causing a rift. When I used to visit, Piera would sit down and drink coffee with us for at least part of the time, telling stories and joining in the conversation. Now he's not around very often at all.

We're having coffee out on the deck another day when Marit tells me that we must go downstairs – Čierggis is pregnant and about to have puppies. Every time I go to

their house of late, there seems to be a dramatic development. For me, this certainly is one. I love this dog, and
I hate knowing that, once again, she is pregnant and
there will be a gaggle of puppies that need homes. It feels
like this is my responsibility, even though it isn't. I am
irritated that dogs like Čierggis keep getting pregnant,
leaving dogs all over the village that weren't cared for or
were destroyed or given to reckless owners.

Not allowing dogs and cats to be neutered and spayed
is official Norwegian policy, not Sámi. In Norway,
getting an animal 'altered' can only be done with a very
good reason, and you must discuss it with the vet. It's
considered animal cruelty, and is in fact illegal unless it
is medically necessary for the good of the animal. This
bothers me to no end because I see all of the animals that
have to suffer for being born. After Rássi went through
her first heat, or season, I was determined to have her
fixed as soon as possible. It seemed as if dogs seven
villages over could smell her, and dogs were constantly
howling into the night outside of my apartment, pining
to procreate with her, peeing on the building so much
that I had to splash buckets of water against the exte-
rior every morning. The dogs fought for dominance, and
things became so bad that I'd have to chuck Rássi in the
Škoda and drive her as far as possible so that she could
pee or poop without being trailed by a group of dogs. She
would cower in the house and was constantly agitated,
and this was only her first heat. I begged the vet in Alta
to alter her, giving the reason that she was terrified when
she came into heat because of the number of dogs and
aggression, and also 'I live in Kautokeino' to put the situation into context for her – almost everyone in the region

is familiar with issue of the many strays in the area. I also cried, out of sheer frustration that it was so difficult to get the surgery. The vet finally consented after much consideration. Rássi was approved, but fixing a dog here involves a full hysterectomy of the dog, a serious surgery at a cost of around £800. After her operation, we spent a few days in a hotel in Alta, because the drive back would have been too difficult while she recovered. I had to feed her painkillers in hamburger meat. It was brutal.

And now, here was Čierggis with another gaggle of puppies, which I was watching her birth in the basement on the same knotted rug where she'd delivered Rássi and her litter. I go home and call Tracy and tell her about the puppies, and that I'm already wondering if I should take one. They would need homes, and Rássi had brought me so much joy. She was also lonely – this was plain.

I wonder aloud if I should take on this extra commitment. I live in an apartment. I travel. Tracy encourages me, pointing out that I'm already into pet ownership with one dog and two cats, so why stop now. I decide that I will adopt one, but I hold off on telling Marit just yet. The puppies haven't even opened their eyes and will need to wean and develop for at least another eight weeks.

My work situation is unresolved, with no end in sight, just as Pattie had suggested. The stress eats at me, and I literally, in turn, eat the stress; it's as if my two new boyfriends are Ben and Jerry. Sensing my anxiety, Gerlinde offers to do a drum journey with me. I lie on the floor, and Gerlinde stands with one of her large handmade drums, beating it steadily for at least an hour. It's something that shamans, not necessarily Sámi, do to enhance a trance state, or in my case, a very deep meditation. In the back of

Gerlinde's house is a *kota*, a small octagonal building with a fire pit in the middle, where we often, no matter the time of year, will sit at the fire as she drums. This is the first time that I've done an actual drum journey, and I'm amazed at how a sense of peace washes over me. Some people report seeing their 'spirit animal' and I can't get the idea of a giant golden eagle out of my head. I tell Gerlinde this afterwards, and she gives me an eagle feather. Soon she'll be going back to Germany for the summer, as she always does, to visit family, and I offer to water her herb gardens while she's away. I will miss her.

Out of nowhere, an email comes from the office of my old boss from the *LA Times*, Shelby. His assistant wants to know if I'm still in Norway because he's coming through on a cruise with his wife, and if so, the assistant asks, how far away is Hammerfest? It's five hours by car, but I don't care at all. Distances like this are nothing in Sápmi, and I haven't seen Shelby in at least four years. I can't think of anyone I'd like to see more at this moment. I get the details of when his ship will dock from his assistant and leave Rássi with Bjarne and Maia and the kids, setting out the next morning.

The trip to Hammerfest is one that ambulance drivers in Kautokeino know well, because it is the location of the nearest hospital. Driving there myself gives me new appreciation for these drivers, in that the journey is simple enough to Skaidi, where I'd taken Rássi the previous summer, but from there, the road turns into a series of twists and turns, heading through villages that hug the sea amid dramatic landscapes. It's easy enough in the summer, but I imagine the EMTs having to do such a drive on icy roads in winter, while simultaneously having to administer medical care. The last part hugs the coast, and as I climb higher and higher through small villages, I'm completely taken by the tableau of red and yellow clapboard barns and houses, so quintessentially Scandinavian, set against the backdrop of blue sky, dramatic ocean vistas and sloping hills of verdant grass dotted with white wildflowers growing with abandon everywhere. It's stunning, and as much as I always describe clouds to be so low in Kautokeino that you could almost touch them, here, on the edge of the sea, you actually could. I drive through the fast-moving low clouds, plumes of white vapour, and finally have to pull over to experience them for myself. I stand outside and marvel that clouds are actually passing over me. Cool, wet, divine. As a little girl, when I flew on planes I had looked out the windows and was obsessed with what it might feel like to fall through a cloud. Now I had some idea, but without the troublesome last bit of crashing to earth and dying.

It was marvellous.

The journey concludes with crossing over the Kvalsund Bridge, the northernmost suspension bridge in the world, and a short while later, the long drive through the Melkøya tunnel, shooting out to Hammerfest. To my left, in the middle of the Norwegian sea, I can see Seiland, the island where many of the reindeer herders that I know are presently, and will be for the summer, with their reindeer, that are transported over at the start of the season from the mainland on a giant barge. I make it to Hammerfest in good time, and have the evening to spend in the town before meeting Shelby; his ship is sailing from fjord to fjord and due to arrive in the morning. I go to a restaurant near my hotel to grab a bite to eat, only to see main courses that are at least £25 – far too extravagant for me. I have a starter and call it a night.

I hear their ship coming in in the morning and can see it docking from my hotel room, all 68,870 tonnes of it, carrying nearly a thousand passengers. I park my Škoda near the berth and board the ship with my passport, necessary for the manifest, and find Shelby and his wife, Mary Lee, waiting.

Shelby gives lectures on cruise ships, related to current events, and this is why they are in my part of the world. I can't get enough of hearing his take on everything that's happening back in America. He is the quintessential newsman. We spend a long lunch catching up, and I'm thrilled to have this time with both of them – I've known Shelby since I was barely eighteen and a copy messenger at the *Times*. I don't let on that anything is troubling me with work – I don't know if he could sense it – but when I am getting ready to leave, Shelby gives me a quick hug and pulls out his wallet. 'Laura, you drove a long way and I know that gas is expensive in Norway. I'd like to give you some money to cover the cost.'

I refuse this generous gesture, but cry halfway home for the grace of it.

*

The puppies' eyes are wide open now and they are everything. During the day, they stay outside in a dog enclosure that has a covered doghouse filled with straw, where Čierggis nurses them. They tumble and frolic and are perfection. I walk over to Marit's every day with

253

Rássi now, just to play with the puppies and monitor their development. Marit had made such a good choice for me with Rássi that I ask her to select my new puppy. She picks a little one that is a carbon copy of Čierggis in colouring, black with some white spots on her paws and underbelly and the tip of her tail. The puppies gleefully pull at Rássi's leash, leading her all over the yard and the house, as Rássi patiently submits.

What to call her? I don't want to call her Čierggis, or Čáhppe, or any of the other traditional Sámi names for dogs. The name that keeps coming forward for me is Nilla, because this puppy shares the same attributes as my favourite childhood cookie in America, Nilla wafers. She is sweet and childlike. I decide this will be her name, and it doesn't occur to me that Nilla is also Sámi for the Norwegian name Nils. You just don't name your dogs after people – this isn't done. I have to explain over and over that she's named after a cookie brand and not a person.

It will still be weeks before she can come home.

Gerlinde is away and Greta is more and more out of my life, a fact that I lament to Marit. Marit explains that this is what happens: she's folded into her life with a herder and there is time for little else or others. I miss her. But Maia is becoming a better and better friend, and we take long hikes around Kautokeino with Rássi. One hike requires driving fifteen kilometres away, to the village of her birthplace, Ávži, and then doing an uphill hike to Bealjášvárri, two mountain peaks that overlook Kautokeino and from which you can see for miles and miles over the tundra: the flowing rivers, the sweeping plains. The actual hike up to the peaks is steep and somewhat treacherous – especially for me, a person who is afraid of heights. Rássi takes the climb with the confidence of a sure-footed mountain goat, her long fur blowing in the wind.

I talk to Maia about anything and everything on these walks. She teaches me the good places to explore, as she is an inveterate hiker, and we usually conclude with a cup of coffee on their veranda, where Bjarne will join us if he's not out fishing or at the petrol station. Rássi has grown to love Bjarne and Maia's kids beyond measure, because when we visit she's sure to get showered with attention.

Áilu appears at my house one evening, out of nowhere, and asks if he can come in to have coffee. I would ordinarily think this a bad idea, given that he is engaged and I'd be worried about what people might say. But I'd heard through local gossip that he and the woman he was with had broken the engagement. My feelings towards Áilu had softened, and I tell him as much over coffee. That I know how difficult it must have been to attempt to fold his life in with someone so naïve about his. I told him that I thought he was brave for this. I cry when I tell him everything I wanted to say, so many emotions spilling out. We agree that we'll always be friends. And Áilu still wants to visit New York. This meeting was a closure that I needed to have with him, although it only came now, four years later.

20

AMERICA

An old client of mine from years ago calls me to see if I will work on a small project for her. She's based in New York and she asks me to come for a meeting. I'm extremely happy for the work and make plans right away for Rássi at the Alta *hundehotell*, a dog kennel near Alta in a village called Tverrelvdalen, because Bjarne and Maia are unavailable. The kennel is owned by an older couple called Åre and Gerd. They take good care of Rássi and Åre always sends me professional-grade photographs of Rássi that he takes on their walks. He doesn't speak English, and when I pick Rássi up or drop her off he always says '*fin hund*', fine dog.

I decide that if I'm passing through New York I should make my way further north to Maine to see my dad and Joan. They're getting older, much older, now in their late eighties. When my father hears that I'm coming, without my asking, he sends some money for travel and, as ever, I'm grateful. I rent a room in a motel a few towns over, as it's summer and everything nearby is booked. Ordinarily I would stay with Jane and Rick, but I haven't talked to them for a few years now, my anger over our exclusion the last time that my father was ill, before I'd moved to Norway, still simmering.

When I visit, Joan is kind, warm even. She wants to see pictures of where I live and takes an interest in my life. I'm in my middle forties and I still pine for these moments of temporary approval. I never know when these moments will happen, only that they have in the past and therefore could again. This is what has always confounded me about Joan: at one moment normal and even, and then without warning a switch flips and you are cast away. It makes me wonder if I have been a terrible daughter, if there is something wrong with me for ever thinking that she had been cruel or abusive. We visit, and it is pleasant. For this I'm glad. But most importantly, I am so happy to see my father there are no words. He's slowing down tremendously, and for the first time, I can see him ageing. He's on a walker now and moves slowly. His hearing has deteriorated.

I'm in my motel room on my last morning in Maine, packing, when my phone rings. It is an unfamiliar number. I pick it up and it's my stepsister Jane. 'Laura, it's Jane. I don't want to alarm you – everything is OK. Your dad had a small heart attack last night and is in the hospital.'

I call the airline, cancel my plane ticket and drive straight to the hospital. I find my dad, who is resting comfortably. The doctors are running tests. He says he feels fine, that he was light-headed the day before. I can't recall the last time I was alone with him. He wants to talk, and talk, and talk, as if we'd never talked before. He tells me mundane but interesting stories of his family in the past, which isn't allowed in Joan's presence; she won't permit it or creates a scene. He tells me about his time in Korea. He tells me he's sorry for everything that happened. So sorry. I am overcome by the frankness and honesty of the exchange, and I am left with a feeling of healing and the ultimate knowledge that, despite it all, my father loves me.

Jane arrives and we look at each other tentatively. I was so angry with her for so long, but at the centre of it all, I love her. I know she's a good person. We sit downstairs in the hospital waiting room and I tell her I'm sorry for having been so angry, and I explain to her how it felt to the Galloways, that we were perpetually cut out of our father's life, that we were replaced. Jane had two daughters and, during the time we'd been estranged, had gone through struggles of her own, and when things fell apart with the two of us, it was too much – something had to go. We drink ice coffee and cry, and laugh, and hug, and Jane insists that I come home and stay with them. I see Rick and it's the same reunion; he's been with my stepsister since I was six years old, and he's effectively my third brother. We sit late into the night talking. Jane had suffered a serious brain injury some years prior due to a viral infection, as a result of which her long-term memory – and her recollections of most of my childhood – was completely wiped away. We talk and she cries again, now understanding with the perspective of a mother. I finally, finally feel seen and acknowledged.

What isn't as easy is the meeting I am to have the next day. Linda comes to the hospital and takes over, a whirling dervish of authority. She checks in loudly with the doctors and nurses, and addresses my father in a sort of talk-yell because he's hard of hearing. This comes off as patronizing and it makes me feel angry and protective of my father.

I have dinner with Jane and Linda afterwards, and things are going well enough: we talk about politics; I tell them about Norway. Things take a turn when I start to talk about Dad and some of the stories he'd told me about his childhood. Much like her mother, Linda shuts it down immediately, for reasons I'll never understand. 'I don't want to talk about the past. Your father hates his family. Your father is a narcissist. Joan is a narcissist.' Jane and I are both taken aback, but in the interest of peacekeeping, the conversation switches topics. I repeat something that I've said many times before and for years: if my father ever needed me, I would move nearer. If Joan ever needed me, I would also move to look after her. 'I have everything under control,' Linda snaps at me. I wish I could tell you how the rest of the conversation went, but my mind went blank after a few moments of verbal assault.

Out of nowhere, Linda spits into a tirade about everything she has done for my father and Joan. She doesn't stop. It is like being mowed down by a machine gun; I have never experienced anything like it. 'You Galloways owe me a debt of gratitude for all I've done,' she hisses. At this point, I'm openly sobbing in the middle of the restaurant. Linda pays the bill and leaves, but I am badly shaken. I sit with Jane in the car, unable to speak. Jane is at a loss as well. 'I have no idea what just happened. Laura, that was awful. You did not deserve that.'

The incident rattles me to my core because when I was younger, I looked up to Linda as if she were the moon and stars. She'd done profoundly good things for me in my life: she connected me to a world far outside Indiana;

she was close and supportive when I'd divorced Richard. This was also when she was telling me never to talk to my parents again. But cross her or don't agree with her, and it's over. I have a terrible epiphany that Linda, who has battled with Joan and everyone in the family all of her life, is her mother's daughter.

My father turns out to be medically sound; he'd had a very small heart attack but with no apparent lasting damage. He's discharged and I bring him back to his retirement community. I say my goodbyes and I return home to the north.

After my trip, I often think about my brothers and stepsisters, and reflect on why I find it so difficult to maintain solid relationships with them. We have all been on the outs with each other at one point or another, sometimes for years at a time. The same is true for all of us with respect to Dad and Joan. And one day while walking with Rássi, shortly after my return, it dawns on me that the reason for this is that we are all in competition for approval. I was so much younger than everyone else in my family that I'd never stopped to consider that my siblings were also, at their cores, just responding in their own ways to their childhoods. Wasn't everyone?

I'd always viewed my siblings as much older adults, and expected them to have their lives in order and have processed all of the various rejections and disappointments; to have moved forward confidently and whole in the world; and perhaps most importantly, as my siblings, to have stood up to the injustice of it all. I know now that this isn't how it works. We are all just trying to work through life the best we can, attempting to navigate our scars and integrate them into workable, productive lives.

This can only happen with time, reflection and a feeling of safety strong enough to wade into deeper waters, the ugly truths, the acknowledgements of our lesser selves and weaker parts. But you cannot be vulnerable without a safety net of love. And you cannot heal without being vulnerable. I hated how our universal desire for a family, and for inclusion, had normalized the terrible things that had happened to the point of almost wiping them from existence or acknowledgement. Linda's words before her tirade rolled like rocks in my head. 'The past is the past,' Linda said curtly, which was convenient for her because her past wasn't stolen from her.

I also realize, for the first time, that I hold anger towards all of my siblings, rightly or wrongly, rationally or not, for not having rescued me. It's not fair or rational and it's not an anger I want to carry any more. The first step for me is acknowledging that I have any anger at all, because this was a feeling not allowed as I grew up. This realization in itself is a triumph of epic proportions. The second step is recognizing *why* I have anger, and that is because I believed no one had ever protected me when I was younger. Had I not been worthy or valuable enough for someone to step forward? I believed that I wasn't, and that's why everything happened as it did. This is how the child's mind processes things; thoughts are baked into parts of their being as they become adults. I recalled something Linda had said to me many times: Joan is a narcissist, and we are not allowed to topple the queen. Narcissists pit people against each other. It's how they maintain power. And we'd all been so desperate for love and acknowledgement, which came from a limited and strategic supply of both, that we would throw each other under the bus or leave each other in the dust in order to have any sort of attention or inclusion or approval.

I start to talk to my brother Will about this on the phone more and more; we have always had a fraught relationship and I want to understand why. He tells me he resented me because when he was sent away Joan adopted me, and I grew up in a home with two parents. I filled him in on what that landscape looked like for me: that I was always reminded of my otherness, meaning that Joan wasn't my mother and did not want to be, and that our mother was someone terrible and broken who just kept having Galloways, and that by virtue of these affiliations I was also broken. These conversations are productive and healing. They further illuminate that it's time to let this all go; it is baggage too heavy to carry one mile longer. It's also dawning on me that the reason no one helped me wasn't because I wasn't worthy of love and connection. It was because for whatever reason – call it chance, or karma, or divine providence – I had found myself in a family that wasn't capable of providing it in any lasting or dependable way. But I had found that love elsewhere, over and over, in other places. And now I was finding it here, in the most unexpected place of all: the Arctic.

21

NILLA

I walk over to Marit's one day and she's made good on her promise to leave; she's gone with the kids, and I don't know if it's for a vacation or longer because we haven't spoken. I find Piera at home with Čierggis and all of the puppies, who are downstairs and have pooped and peed and made a mess of things. They're hungry. I tell him I'll look after them, and I go to the pet store in Alta and buy weaning dog food and then to the pharmacist to get incontinence bed pads, a much cheaper alternative to puppy wee pads. I clean up the downstairs and feed all the pups, coming back every day to make sure they're fed and watered. Homes have been found for most of the dogs now; they will be good herding dogs and are going for a lot of money a piece. I'm taken aback by this and I don't have the money to spare to pay for Nilla – I hadn't considered that she'd be sold to me. But without my saying a word, Piera speaks. 'Laura, you've done a lot to help. I can't take money because of it. I am giving you your dog.'

When the other dogs are taken by their new owners, Nilla is left with one other puppy at the house, and Piera, who must attend to something else, asks me to come over and stay for the morning until the dog is collected. It's still a week early, in theory, for these dogs to be away from Čierggis, but there's no one to look after them. A woman picks up the remaining puppy and I leave with Nilla, the newest member of our family. I love her so.

My new neighbour upstairs is called Dagmar, and her grandchildren, two little girls who live up the street, love cats. They've heard about Boo and one day there's a knock at my door and they ask in Sámi if they can see him. They enter my apartment, tentative and wide-eyed, as if they've never seen the strange and unusual lair of an American. They play with the cats and are captivated by tiny Nilla. I pull out some crayons and colouring books that I have on hand for visitors with kids. They sit at my kitchen table and colour and then leave. The next day they come back with two more kids, one of whom is around eight years of age and says, 'Hello. I speak English and I will be the translator.' She starts asking me all manner of questions, which are more a function of showing off her language skills than anything else. 'How old are the cats?' 'How old are the dogs?' 'What is your favourite food?' She translates the answers to the others with a great air of authority. I find it difficult not to burst out in giggles.

Dagmar has already been living upstairs for more than a year. The time has flown. I've finished my master's thesis and am awaiting a grade; I have spare time now. I walk one street over to Tildá's to visit on occasion; the house is crammed from wall to wall with stuff – bursting, really. She has a very large yard that is overrun with tall grasses and weeds, an Eden for mosquitos. It would be gorgeous if the grass were mown. One day I visit her with Rássi and Nilla in tow. Nilla, after watching Boo on many occasions, immediately spots a litter box in the corner of the living room, promptly steps into it, poops and covers it up.

As we sit and have coffee, Tildá tells me that she's leaving Kautokeino and is going to move south. It feels as if everyone I know is departing. She wants to know if I want the house; she will put in a good word with the owner, a Swedish woman who lives on the other side of the village with her boyfriend. I ask about the rent and quickly calculate that, with the return of the deposit on my apartment, this would be cheaper than where I'm presently living, and it would give the animals a surfeit of space. So many people are looking for rentals like this that I'm taken aback by Tildá's generosity and kindness in letting me know first and offering to suggest me.

I speak with the landlord, called Inga, and she agrees to rent me the place, but I'll have to give it a fresh coat of paint; she will set to work on the other tasks needed to bring the house up to standard.

Bjarne comes with his flatbed trailer to haul things to the dump for Tildá – at least five full loads leave the house. A very nice couple from the south, friends of Tildá's, agree to adopt Guvge, as Tildá can't walk far and she's moving into an apartment. I meet them and both Bjarne and I are thrilled, because the man is a runner, and Guvge will finally get the exercise and attention he needs. They also clearly adore him, and I know he'll be well taken care of. This dog has been a favourite of both of ours, and Bjarne gets a frog in his throat when they drive away with Guvge looking back at us. I cry hysterically.

When Áilu left, all that time ago, he'd also left all of the furniture and the contents of the apartment behind;

they had all been donated by family and friends. Now I am trying to track down the provenance of each item, but no one seems to want their things back – most of it is threadbare and completely falling apart – so I ask Áilu to help haul it to the dump a few kilometres away. I want the new place to be open and spare. I keep only a simple pine dining table and a couple of bookshelves, and get a new bed, with the idea to add more furniture later when things are more flush. We take the things to the dump together, and I go to see the empty house that is waiting for me.

Inga, her daughter and her boyfriend are working like crazy on the new house; after finding stains and animal pee under the floorboards, they have laid new floors and cut the grass. They've even planted flowers in the front. The house is transformed.

I need to figure out a solution for the dogs, though, who need a fenced yard. I'm taken aback by the price of fencing, which costs much more than anything I might have saved by moving to the house. This is a serious problem, and I worry about it for days, until Bjarne calls me to say he's read on Facebook that a sheep farmer is selling fencing and posts, and has opened the sale of these items to online bidding. Also, the fencing must be picked up that night. 'No problem!' says Bjarne.

Thanks to Bjarne's guidance, I win the bid, getting the fencing for a fraction of what I would have paid for it anywhere else. Bjarne shows up at my house with his trailer hitched up, and we make the drive to Alta. I tell him that I need to find a 'luftfuckter' if we have time on the way back. Bjarne nearly runs off the road, he is laughing so hard – he hears me saying 'air fucker' but knows what I really meant to describe: a small fan that one sets on top of the log burner to distribute the warm air.

We reach the farm by nightfall and quickly load the poles and the fencing into the flatbed. The farmer hears my accent and asks if I'm the woman from America with the white dog.

'Yes, that's me!' I respond.

He tells me his uncle is Åre, the owner of the *hunde-hotell*. 'He likes the dog very much!' he says. 'Here, take a door for your fence, too!'

We make it back to Kautokeino late at night, and next comes the task of putting the fence up. If ever there is a job for a reindeer herder, it is this. Áilu has been helping me paint the house and he, along with some others, also helped me move my things. Now he is tackling the fence. The poles are eight feet high, and he goes from pole to pole, ramming them into the hard earth with a speed and precision that's astonishing. He then wraps the fencing around each of the poles, and he and Bjarne staple them in place.

I now have one of the largest dog enclosures in the village. I go to the local cable company and ask after the large wooden spools used for wrapping cable, many of which sit outside of the office, empty. It turns out that one of Áilu's brothers-in-law, a Norwegian, is the manager of the company. He agrees to give me a spool, and even delivers it to the house; I cut out the middle and fill the inside with straw and have a cosy doghouse.

I'm delighted to learn more about my neighbours. Across the street is a Sámi photographer nicknamed Proffen. When I'd first moved to Kautokeino, he'd asked me if I wanted to assist him; he needed help moving his photography gear. His car was filled with camera equipment and radios and tracking devices for finding the auroras. Auroras are ephemeral, and when we caught a glimpse of them in the distance, we jumped in the car and sped down the pockmarked road leading to an abandoned mine to get out of the light pollution, quickly setting up camera equipment on the tundra to capture the spectacular panoply of green aurorae that danced across the sky, set against a thousand twinkling stars in the crisp, dark night sky. A bit of an artist, at one point Proffen inexplicably had me hold a giant painting of Che Guevara under the auroras. It was weird and unexpected and I loved it. I am happy to know that he is now my neighbour. Down the street is an older man named Totti, whom I'd met at his brother's sixtieth birthday party at their family farm near Karasjok some years back. Totti is also Bernt Morten's best friend, and he has a small Papillon dog named Slurfi, who might only be the size of a small cat, but traverses the neighbourhood as if he is actually a Great Dane. He is fearless.

*

We are settling into our new home, me and the animals, tucked in for another winter. Money is terribly tight, although I am making do by proofreading and cleaning up the English for a Sámi professor in some of his journal articles. A dear friend of mine, a successful technology entrepreneur in America, knows about the trouble I've gone through with my former client and steps in to advise me and also throws me a lifeline until things are resolved; I am astounded by his generosity. Things are uncertain, but I feel supported and more and more a part of the community, in that I am really in a routine and have friends here. I am cosy; in the living room is the biggest stand-alone black cast-iron oven you could imagine, so old that it isn't sold in stores or even made any more. If you light a fire and feed it wood, the whole house will be toasty warm within minutes.

The house is also central. I have a car, but scarcely need it now.

The small one-roomed store in the centre of the village that used to be called COOP has shut down, now replaced by a giant grocery store that sits adjacent to the football field. I hated the store at first because it had come at the cost of a large patch of nature being razed. But it's just down the street from my new place, making it easy to get to and from the store in only a short walk.

It's on one of these walks that the dog I'd kept warm in my apartment appears and follows me past the automatic doors and into the store, so that I have to shoo him out and leave. He's freezing, and he follows me home. I give him shelter for the night; Rássi and Nilla like him, and he seems to be fine with the cats. I feed all the dogs and he drinks a full bowl of water and then sleeps heavily in front of the fire. In the morning I let him out, just as I had done in the old apartment.

He starts to follow us on walks, and then his owner appears, a woman named Magga, who is with a reindeer herder. I tell her that I don't mind the dog coming along with us. I hear her say his name is Runne as she calls him to jump in the car. I let her know where we live in case she can't find him again.

I tell Bjarne about Runne and he corrects me. 'Nei, nei – his name is *Ranne*, not *Runne*.'

'No, Bjarne, it's Runne,' I insist. We go back and forth.

'*Okei!* He is Ranne Runne!' Maia laughs, and from this point forward, this is how we refer to him. Ranne Runne comes to my place frequently, as if he's a third dog of mine. I don't mind at all.

As Christmas festivities begin, the annual Jul quiz, or Christmas quiz, takes place above the local pub, Alfred's Kro. People form teams and answer trivia questions. Mikko G calls me and asks me to be on his team, along with a few others. A man at the front of the room holds a microphone and asks what I find to be difficult questions like 'When was Microsoft founded?' and obscure music trivia. I am never on a winning team, but it's always fun to sit and try. With school out and most businesses celebrating their *julebord*, work Christmas dinners, the holidays have begun, and quiz night is usually the beginning of holiday party nights for people without children.

I still can't bring myself to go out late alone. I'm too self-conscious. These moments remind me that I'm lonely, in the sense that I'd like to be with a partner. It's also difficult for me to get used to the Norwegian style of dating, which is totally opposite to my Midwestern upbringing. In Norway, the norm seems to be that you sleep with someone first and then decide if you want to date, something that was utterly shocking to me when a female friend first explained it. She was in turn shocked by my way of thinking, which was that it was important to get to know someone first. 'Why would you want to date someone if you do not know you're compatible in "that" way, right away?' she asked me, honestly perplexed. And I suppose she had a point. But it made me wonder if I would ever find a partner here who was right for me.

22

WILD

In the spring, when everything is starting to melt with wild abandon, the Kautokeino river becomes the temporary resting spot for the most magnificent surprise of nature. Every year, dozens and dozens of pairs of regal white tundra swans arrive for the summer to nest, fattening up before moving on to North America, where they'll winter.

Along with all of the other birds and animals giving birth, there is an explosion of sparrows around the village, and my house is an area of high danger, in that Rennie the cat also goes outside and, much to my dismay, is a capable and prolific bird killer. Boo sticks mostly to field mice, having apparently become an expert in this kind of hunting during his months away, so I am also constantly finding mice on the doorstep or just over the threshold. I read somewhere that cats don't bring mice in as gifts, as I was always led to believe, but as a way of trying to show humans they like how to hunt. Boo must think I'm an abysmal hunter; he even left me a mouse on the kitchen counter on one occasion. I love animals but am squeamish about dead ones, and finding them startles me every single time.

Occasionally Rennie will leave a bird half-alive, which is distressing both to the bird and to me. One day, I find a little bird at my doorstep that is very much alive but wounded. I bring it in the house and put it in a box with some straw, seed and water. It eats a bit and drinks. I don't know what to do, so I call Tracy in America, as she's an avid bird lover and also rescues pigeons. She connects me to a rehabilitation rescue in New York called the Wild Bird Fund; I call them because there is no resource like this that I know of in the north. I talk to the director of the rescue and she tells me that it is very likely the bird won't live because the bite probably gave it an infection. She advises that I euthanize it, for the good of the bird.

There is no way I can do this. Bjarne is a bird lover and I know that he won't either, so I call another friend of mine, a very kind Sámi man named Andres Per, who is a social worker at the local community centre. I ask him if he would come over to help me with the bird, a task I know he is up to because he's also a hunter. He arrives at my house to see the little sparrow in a box, and I know it's difficult for him not to laugh because I am fretting so much over a tiny bird. But I don't want him to break its neck – I decide that would be cruel – and so I send him home, thanking him for stopping by and apologizing for wasting his time. I contemplate what do and, instead of letting his neck be broken, I quickly submerge him in water and he dies instantly. I am filled with guilt and remorse for many days later. I bury him in the back yard and say a prayer, cover the grave with flowers; this is the start of my wild animal graveyard, where all the mice and birds are laid to rest.

I read about how to deflect cats from birds, and begin

to understand how destructive outdoor cats are to natural environments, specifically bird populations. Rennie and Boo not going outside is no longer an option, but I find another solution: a special collar has been developed by a company in America which fits around an ordinary cat collar. It is cloth, and it looks exactly like a clown's neck ruffle. These collars are colourful with special patterns designed by scientists that are supposed to be recognized by birds and alert them to stay away. I order some and put them on the cats, who now look like clown cats with their jaunty new accessories. They don't mind them at all; the only problem is that it looks to people in the village as if I've now really lost the plot – the American lady who has reverted to dressing up her cats. With the collars, Rennie never catches another bird again, nor does Boo. Now the only fear is that the birds might instead laugh themselves to death.

One of the hottest summers on record comes to Kautokeino; the land is dry and brittle and you can feel the moss crackle under your feet as you walk the tundra.

There is a little stretch of sandy beach along parts of the river to the south of the village where people go every day to dip in the water and stay cool. The area quickly gets the nickname 'Kautokeino Riviera' and people come wearing bikinis and toting plastic blow-up lounging rafts. I go often with Rássi and Nilla, as this kind of heat is too much for the dogs, and they spend hours swimming joyfully in the cool Arctic water. I go to the beach with Bjarne and Maia and the kids, Sunna Mari's perfect milk-white skin now tinged with the sting of red sunburn. It is a languid summer of dry heat and long walks and mostly pyrrhic efforts to cool off.

A hard reality is starting to set in for me; it has been creeping up for the last year. It pains me to think about leaving Kautokeino or the north: this is a place that I love deeply and it has become part of my heart. It has given me the space to reflect and taught me so many things. But I need to start thinking seriously about my working future. I need a job, and I need to build stability. The last several years have been a rollercoaster, and I'm getting to an age at which I can't take more risks; I am on my own. I've now been in the Arctic for five years. When I was working on the project that went sideways, I was often asked if I would consider moving to London. It is a place I've always wanted to live, as far as cities go; but for now, I need to focus on finding a job anywhere one might become available. I need to be aggressive in my search, knowing that it will take time. It kills me to think of leaving this place, but it's becoming more and more apparent that the long-term prospects for work here or from here are non-existent. I'm also too far away to keep consulting: it is impossible to generate new clients from such a distance. It is also exhausting trying to constantly keep my head above water working for myself.

When I start my search, I don't know if it's that I've changed, or the world has changed, or both, but I am astonished by how impersonal and defeating job-seeking has become. I send out several responses to job postings on LinkedIn and other sites, taking time to write detailed and thoughtful cover letters. No responses come, and then my friend Adam explains that there are now algorithms that read CVs, and if you don't have your CV calibrated, it simply gets overlooked. I contact recruiters who are enthusiastic and promising and want to talk 'right away', and then nothing. I talk to good recruiters; I talk to more than a few terrible ones. I apply for work in London with a non-profit that has engaged an external recruitment agency. I feel as if I have a fairly good shot because a close friend is also a former colleague of and advisor to the non-profit's director. My friend writes a glowing endorsement, but everyone is shuffled through the recruiter, who must be on the early side of nineteen and just out of school. She asks me questions as if running through a script, like 'What do you consider your key leadership abilities?' 'Can you discuss times in which you have had to solve difficult problems?' I am waiting for her to ask me 'What colour is your parachute?' before the interview ends. I get a pro forma rejection letter the next day, via email, saying I'm not right for the job because I don't have enough international experience. Old Laura would have cowered and accepted this answer, but recently-empowered-by-five-years-of-self-examination-and-shame-shedding-on-the-Arctic-tundra Laura had moulted into something different and more confident. I emailed her back and asked for a second call, in which I asked why this would be the reason not to advance in the search, given that I had an overseas master's degree and had worked frequently on global projects in the UK, Europe, India and Africa. She was clearly at a loss and apologized, flustered. I did not get the job and did not expect to at that point, but I wanted it to be on fair evaluation and not an incorrect conclusion. I talk to Adam and then other friends in their forties and fifties about job searches in the current environment in which technology rules and people are data, coupled with the outrageous and impersonal rudeness of the process; I hear horror stories of people going through months-long evaluations for jobs and being asked to do numerous writing samples or presentation tests without being paid, only to not get the role. In my worst experience, an old and very respected mentor of mine connects me to a company on whose advisory board he sits. I am asked to do eight different interviews with eight separate people, as well as fly to London for a meeting, in all of which everyone is enthusiastic and encouraging, only for it to go nowhere. I call my mentor and ask him if I had mis-stepped at any point; he checks around and discovers that it was simply a case of no one seeing making a new hire as a priority, and so it fell by the wayside.

Defeating job searches aside, I also decide that I am ready to be in a relationship again. I need to look towards the future in my personal life as well. Despite the community I've grown to love, and my friends here, I would like to find a partner; I've been alone for years now, and feel as if my heart has healed from my past experiences, and I'm finally ready to walk into a relationship clear headed, knowing myself better. Because I often travel to the UK for meetings, I sign up for an online dating site there and am clear about where I live – my dating profile even has a picture of me wrapped up in my winter clothing. I get responses from a variety of men; most are adventure seekers, which, despite living in the Arctic, really isn't my type. I talk to a couple of them in messages, and one over Skype, but nothing is clicking, and I don't hold out much hope.

*

I love absolutely everything about fall, and welcome its approach even more after the hot summer that has just passed. Now the leaves are turning and brisk breezes sweep across the tundra. This is the time for gathering from the earth, reaping from the thick blanket of berries that spreads across the land. There are blueberries and crowberries, a black berry that grows low on the ground and is most abundant; these are filled with vitamin C and are excellent eaten by the handful straight off the bush or pressed into a juice with a little sugar added. Rássi and Nilla love crowberries, and they stop and graze on them when we're walking, faces nuzzled in the carpet of green. There are also red *tyttebær*, known in English as lingon-berries, which boiled with water and a bit of sugar make a staple sauce that goes with reindeer and potatoes. I go out with big buckets and spend hours collecting, washing and freezing the berries for winter. Mushrooms are also in abundance but I'm afraid to delve deep into mushroom picking because of the possibility of accidentally eating something poisonous. One day Maia goes mushroom picking with me, as she is an expert, and even has a little mushroom-picking kit with a small knife and brush to gingerly dust off dirt from the caps, gills and stems. She has a small illustrated reference book and shows me pictures, and I start to hunt for mushrooms with her, depositing them in a cloth rucksack. I pick a mushroom I haven't seen before. 'That is fine – you just need to boil that one for a couple of hours to get the toxins out,' Maia says cheerfully. With no offence to Maia and her culinary daring, I dump it in my yard when I get home, too scared to take a chance.

It's cold enough to light fires, and now Ranne Runne is always at my house; it's as if I have three dogs. As luck would have it, his owners have moved down the street from me – they know where he is and it's OK that he comes to my house. Occasionally Magga or Ole the reindeer herder, his owners, will appear, and tell me that it is time for Ranne Runne to work, and then he's gone for periods herding, always returning thinner from running the vast tundra.

The new grocery store near my house has an abundance of food; too much, like the Whole Foods in London. Someone there usually gives me some of the stale bread that can't be sold for the magpies and crows, which seem to know me now and wait for me to come out and feed them in the mornings. The rest of the unsold food is thrown into a giant locked dumpster each week. There is *so much* waste. There is such an excess of meat and other perishable food that goes unsold that it is put in a big refrigerator case towards the back of the store a day or two before it expires and is usually 50 per cent off or more. The idea of an animal being killed in factory farming only to be thrown in the trash for non-use horrifies me, so I try to only buy meat if it is in the case and would otherwise go to waste. This is how I feed the dogs; I cook all of their food, and so they eat lamb and cooked chicken and good quality beef mixed with vegetables and a bit of kibble. Amazingly, it's a cheaper way to feed them, and Ranne Runne is filling out. I love this dog; when we are not at home he will sit for hours outside the house waiting for us to return. Rássi and Nilla treat him as one of the pack.

One evening I get a new contact from the dating site and log on to see a message from a new man; I click through and see his picture. It says that he's athletic and enjoys sports with his kids; he looks like a jock, but he is also an artist. He's handsome, and he's holding an adorable dog in his picture. I respond to his message, and we begin to correspond. He is very different from me on the surface, but I'm intrigued by him, and we message each other more and more. I tell him I live in the Arctic but come to London often; he tells me he is a busy lawyer and doesn't travel much. Soon I find myself telling him things about myself I would never tell anyone and waiting for replies to my messages. Something is growing.

My birthday comes around and I decide to do something with the *tyttebær* I've been picking all fall. I bake two sponges from scratch and make a *tyttebær* layer cake with cream and *tyttebær* rolled in sugar. I invite Bjarne and Maia and Gerlinde and a few others over. They have been incredible friends to me through so many learning curves and difficulties. I'm grateful beyond measure for all of them.

We sit and have cake and coffee and talk for hours. The cake isn't very good because I've put too much sugar in it and its grainy, but no one says anything, even Gerlinde, who doesn't eat sugar at all but is being polite. Gerlinde made me a bracelet for my birthday, a string of hearts on a silver chain. She puts it in my hand. 'It's a bracelet of hearts because you have such a big heart,' she says.

And then Nils Åke and Sunna Mari hand me a card, which is handmade with pictures of all of us through the seasons. Next to the reindeer with which Áilu had gifted me all those years ago, it is the most precious gift I've ever been given. It reads, in Sámi, Norwegian and English:

'We wish you a happy birthday, you are a good person, helpful and kind, but you can also point out the message when needed. You are now a person from Guovdageadinu, you care about animals, nature and environment. You are not afraid of tasting bog blueberries, even if someone tricked you and said they were poisonous. We love you.'

I can't help but cry openly I am so overwhelmed. I also wonder if they sense that I am starting to think about going. It is a quiet knowingness, this gift of prescience that many of the people from the north have, and one that only comes from silence and nature and the stillness of this place, a place that is singular.

23

RETURN

I take another trip back to the United States to visit my family; things have improved dramatically since the healing of the previous year. I stay with Jane and Rick at their house, and we spend many hours talking. I even see Linda; I am still trying to figure out how to interact with her without getting hurt, but every time I see her, I remember the parts of her that I appreciate – her intelligence, for example.

I spend a lot of time reflecting on how much of our behaviour is dictated by things that happened to us as kids; and in thinking about this, I try and picture the most hurtful people I know as children, imagining them as that, rather than the adults they've become. I know how much of my own life has been shaped and defined by the hurt, loss, rejection and aloneness I'd felt as a child, and how much I'd played that scenario out in adult relationships with people who had done nothing to hurt or alienate me. I was trying hard to forgive myself for living out that pattern and to have active forgiveness for those who'd also lived it out on me. Hardest of all was to muster that empathy for Joan, but if I think of her as a child, I wonder what terrible things may have occurred to make her feel so threatened and controlling and to carry it into adulthood, spraying shards of destruction in every direction. I imagine her now as a scared child, and I try hard to think of her with love for the things that she did give me: an appreciation for the world and the skill of independence, although the latter was imposed rather than gifted. There were moments that I saw her love me, when the armour fell; and I know for this reason she is likely not a bad person at her core, just damaged into another shape entirely. I want to believe that almost everyone is redeemable; the hard part is being vulnerable enough to love and be loved, not knowing what might come back.

I have been talking to Jonathan, the man I met online, for nearly three months now, non-stop. We Skype every day and talk every night, and he sends me his artwork: amazing pen and inks that are complex and mysterious and seem to come from a place deep inside him. Although he is a lawyer by day, he is truly an artist. I have never met anyone in my life to whom I have felt so connected at such a soul level. I still have not met him in person, but I feel as if I have known him forever. This nascent love feels fearless and profound.

I have a work trip to London where I meet him for the first time. I arrive and check in to the hotel first, waiting nervously for him to appear. He opens the door of the hotel and my heart swells. He is classically handsome, with wavy brown hair that is starting to grey slightly, fine features and the kindest eyes. He is measured and steady, reflective when he speaks and patient when he listens. He is fit, the product of a life spent regimenting himself through sports and running. I am also relieved to find that he stands an inch taller than I do. Not that it matters much. I know already that I would have loved this man at any height, in any condition.

I need to return to the Arctic, and for now he's busy with work and his two boys, with whom he shares custody with his ex-wife. I visit London when I can, and Jonathan makes his way up to the Arctic. He meets Maia and Bjarne and Gerlinde and we sit and have coffee in Gerlinde's *kota* around the fire. They all like him very much. The animals love him as well, which is an essential confirmation.

One night, it is forty below and we are preparing dinner when out the window I see the whisper of some auroras outside. I tell Jonathan to grab his jacket and bundle up quickly, and we run out and observe the most spectacular auroras I've seen since living in the north. I'm unlikely ever to see them in such brilliance again: vivid wavering greens and silky whites, dancing in glorious streaks across the sky, intensifying and lingering. It is a one in a million night.

The winter rapidly turns into spring, and in late summer, after much discussion, I make the decision to go and stay in the UK with Jonathan for six months – the time allowed for a visitor's visa.

I don't know what the future will hold there, but the decision feels right and important to explore. I don't want to fly; this would be unmanageable with all the animals. I have my Škoda looked at, and it's in good condition. The mechanic is confident that this more-than-a-decade-old car will easily make it, with a few adjustments and a new set of tyres.

I set about checking the rules for pet entry – thankfully, all of the animals have pet passports, and Norway has some of the strictest animal welfare requirements on earth, so all of my pets are up to date on their shots and have international microchips. I will keep the house in Norway for the time being, until I have a clearer sense of what direction the future will take.

Boo is sensing that something is up; three days before I am set to start driving, he disappears. I email Tim Link, the pet psychic, and ask him if he can locate Boo. He's been gone for two days, and this has not happened for a few years, not since his last adventure. I get an email back from Tim fifteen minutes later. He describes Boo's location, a house three doors down, in specific detail. 'I've made contact with Boo and told him you're looking for him. I've asked him to come home immediately.' Within five minutes, Boo is meowing at the front door.

I'm worried about Ranne Runne; we are set to leave while he's away with the reindeer and he won't know what's happened. I go to Alta and buy food and chew bones and a new collar for him, and leave them with Magga. I tell her I'll be back, but I want her to have these things for him. I stay extra prayers for Ranne Runne and hope that I'll see him when I return.

In the meantime, I have a course to plot across Europe: drive times, hotels that take pets, car insurance. The trip will take me 3,292 kilometres across seven countries, with two cats and two dogs. I need to be prepared.

AFTERWORD

I walk Rássi and Nilla down airport road for the last time, overcome with emotion. I thank the earth, the sky, the nature for all that it's given me.

For the past six years, this place has been both my teacher and my refuge. It has offered difficult lessons; it has offered the greatest gifts.

It has also taught me the most powerful lesson of all: I am loved.

I will miss it so.

I know now that home is not a physical place; it is not a destination at which one arrives by ship or train. Home is inside you and all around you, but not in a brick and mortar sense. Home is with the people who surround and love you unconditionally, no matter the distance or location. It is the invisible power of the connections and friendships and bonds that you make, strengthening what's inside of you, whispering 'I am here' when you are most alone. Home makes you part of something; home is built not with planks or bricks or shingles, or blood and bones, but with love, understanding and empathy.

Every road led me to this place, but it was only in the silence of nature that the realization emerged that, for my whole life, love has been in ambush everywhere, stepping out always, just when I needed it.

*

Ranne Runne is still away, and this is the one goodbye that lingers in my heart. Hours before I lock up the house to go, I catch a glimpse of Bjarne outside, kneeling with Rássi, whispering to her. 'I love you, girl,' he says, over and over.

I do not know if I will return to this place to live again. But before I go, I say a prayer to it: to the land and the people and this place that held me close.

*

I pack the car with the animals and we drive towards the Finnish border, and then through to Sweden and all the way down the length of the country, which takes three days and two nights of driving straight, fourteen hours a day. We take short breaks along the way. The animals are amazingly serene for the trip; at night we stop in hotels and I set up food and water and a litter box and they sleep and eat and stretch. The dogs get long walks. Our journey takes us through Finland, Sweden, Denmark, Germany, the Netherlands, Belgium and France, where the animals are checked for entry in Calais. It occurs to me that Rennie and Boo may be the most travelled cats on the planet at this point. We take the car train under the English Channel, and finally emerge in England. I am amazed that my car has made it; but it got us here, and safely.

Jonathan is waiting for us all.

I do not yet know what the future holds, but knowing I've found the meaning of home, anything is possible.

ACKNOWLEDGMENTS

I'm incredibly grateful for the many people who have entered my life as friends and teachers over the years. This includes my entire family, whom above all else, I hold in love for the journey we've taken together.

I'd like to say thank you to all those who helped guide this book, starting with my agent, Jim Levine, of Levine Greenberg Rostan Literary Agency, Michael Nardullo and the rest of the team at LGR. Massive thanks to my United Kingdom co-agent, Anna Carmichael at Abner Stein, for doggedly representing this book until it found exactly the right home with Allen & Unwin. Thank you also to Sandy Violette and Cristela Henriquez at Abner Stein, who have been so skilled in guiding me through all the practicalities surrounding book publishing.

I'm very grateful to my editor, Clare Drysdale, who gave this book life and direction, and me courage, with the added benefit of my having made a wonderful friend along the way. Working with you, Clare, has been a complete pleasure. My thanks also to Emma Dunne for her copy editing work, and everyone at Allen & Unwin, for showing this first-time author how a book is created and making the process joyful and interesting.

Several people helped with early reads of the book and its various parts. Thank you to Mark Jobling, Professor of Genetics at the University of Leicester, and Heather A. Zierhut, Associate Professor and Genetic Counselor at the University of Minnesota, for their review and feedback on my scientific explanations; to Maia Hætta, for her careful review and corrections of my Sámi spellings and impressions; and to Molly Schiever, for her keen editing skills, astute observations and her extraordinary friendship, which included (and still does) not only listening to me ruminate for hours on end, but for providing me with a welcoming and peaceful place in which to finish the book. You are cherished.

I could take up twenty pages listing all of the wonderful souls at the *Los Angeles Times* who made my time there some of the best years of my life, resulting in many lifelong friendships that I treasure to this day. And so much laughter! My deepest thanks to all of you who were around in that extraordinary early 1990s period.

Thank you to all the wonderful women (and man!) of Supercuts, including Carol, Kristy, Mary, Kim Taylor Browning, Gail Strejc and Marc Port, and to my late and dear Café Espresso friends, Bill O'Keefe and Richard Howell, who were also my protectors and who taught me so much and are still very much alive in my thoughts. And thank you to Warren Kelly, who meant so much to my siblings and me.

To Natalie Pechacek, Carol Verbeke-Fountain, Janice Milgrim and Sophie Weber, who through the years have been wise and loving mother figures when needed, which was a lot of the time. Thank you for always being there regardless of time and distance. And to Paul, Tracy,

Michael L., Jill, Joe, Alex, Dennis and Ezequiel, you will never know what your friendships have meant to me. Thank you for your love, support, guidance, laughter and wisdom in all kinds of weather. To you all: we might not share blood and bones, but you are family.

To Louise Woods, Pattie Canova, Claudia Handler, Joe Addeo and Michael Lutin, thank you for lighting my path over the years and inspiring me to always look deeper. You all have been a gift, and I've learned so much from each of you. Thank you.

To Rob Asghar, Michelle Floan, James Duncan Davidson, Alan Citron, Shelby Coffey, Paul Yonover, Emily McManus, Bruno Guissani, Lara Stein, Henrik and Eva Åhlen, Carl Mossfeldt, Linda Zachrison, Alexander Crawford, David Gallagher, Jonathan Weber, Kathleen Craughewell, Ed Hoffman, Deborah Scranton, Herbert Milgrim, Lesly Deschler-Canossi, Bob Thurman, Mark Stevenson, Caroline Smith and Natasha Dantzig, thank you for your ongoing friendship. Your presence in my life has made a difference.

And to my friends in Norway — most especially Stein, Maia, Bjarne, Gerlinde, Bernt Morten, Stine, Harrieth, Katarina, Susanne, Lisbeth, Mikko and Per E. — thank you for always so generously helping me navigate a totally new world, and for being treasured and wonderful friends, really the best in the world. I'm truly grateful for each of you.

And to Åshhild, who might be very surprised to find herself in the acknowledgments of this book — your friendliness during small and simple exchanges at the market, over and over for a period of years, lifted me often and during some of my most alone days. You taught me this lesson: be kind always...you never know how needed that kindness may be.

Sámi álbmogii, ja erenoamážit Guovdageaidnolaččaide, giitu. Dii lehpet álo mu váimmus.

And finally, to Jonathan, to whom this book is dedicated and without whose love, understanding and support this book would never have been written. No words seem adequate other than to say thank you. You are magnificent in every way. I love you.